Sinister Wisdom 123
Winter 2022

Publisher: Sinister Wisdom, Inc.

Editor & Publisher: Julie R. Enszer

Guest Editors: Cheryl Clarke, Shromona Mandal

Graphic Designer: Nieves Guerra

Copy Editor: Amy Haejung

Board of Directors: Roberta Arnold, Tara Shea Burke, Cheryl Clarke, Julie R. Enszer, Sara Gregory, Shromona Mandal, Joan Nestle, Rose Norman, Mecca Jamilah Sullivan, Yasmin Tambiah, and Red Washburn

Front Cover Art: Photograph of the *Conditions* editorial collective, courtesy of **Elly Bulkin**.

Back Cover Art: Photograph of *Conditions* editorial collective members marching in New York City, courtesy of **Elly Bulkin**.

SINISTER WISDOM, founded 1976

Former editors and publishers:

Harriet Ellenberger (aka Desmoines) and Catherine Nicholson (1976–1981)

Michelle Cliff and Adrienne Rich (1981–1983)

Michaele Uccella (1983–1984)

Melanie Kaye/Kantrowitz (1983–1987)

Elana Dykewomon (1987–1994)

Caryatis Cardea (1991–1994)

Akiba Onada-Sikwoia (1995–1997)

Margo Mercedes Rivera-Weiss (1997–2000)

Fran Day (2004–2010)

Julie R. Enszer & Merry Gangemi (2010–2013)

Julie R. Enszer (2013–)

Copyright © 2022 *Sinister Wisdom*, Inc.
All rights revert to individual authors and artists upon publication.
Printed in the U. S. on recycled paper.

Subscribe online: www.SinisterWisdom.org
Join *Sinister Wisdom* on Facebook: www.Facebook.com/SinisterWisdom
Follow *Sinister Wisdom* on Instagram: www.Instagram.com/sinister_wisdom
Follow *Sinister Wisdom* on Twitter: www.twitter.com/Sinister_Wisdom
Sinister Wisdom is a US non-profit organization; donations to support the work
and distribution of *Sinister Wisdom* are welcome and appreciated. Consider in-
cluding *Sinister Wisdom* in your will.

Sinister Wisdom, 2333 McIntosh Road, Dover, FL 33527-5980 USA

TABLE OF CONTENTS

NOTES FOR A MAGAZINE

Over a decade ago, I emailed Cheryl Clarke, an icon of mine who, until the moment of my email, I only knew on the page. I was doing early research into my work on lesbian print culture and I had spent time at the Schomburg Center for Research in Black Culture at the New York Public Library where some of Cheryl Clarke's papers are. I learned tantalizing bits about *Conditions* on that research trip, and I emailed Dr. Clarke to ask her if there were additional papers about *Conditions*. She replied, *yes*. There were papers and boxes and boxes of back issues. She presented the option that I could look at the papers IF I helped her place the back issues and end a nearly twenty-year relationship with the storage unit she had rented for all these *Conditions* boxes.

A month or two later I was motoring up to Jersey City to meet her, see these papers, and pick up these boxes. I spent a transformative afternoon with her learning more about *Conditions* and then cramming boxes and boxes of books into the back of a Honda Insight. I drove away that afternoon feeling lucky about the experiences that life brings.

Now nearly fifteen years later, I continue to feel lucky: I get to work with Cheryl Clarke on *Sinister Wisdom* and at times dare to consider her a friend. Even more fortunate for everyone reading this issue, Cheryl worked with Shromona Mandal and me to create this extraordinary tribute to the journal *Conditions*. *Sinister Wisdom* 123: *Tribute to* Conditions demonstrates a fundamental value of mine and of my editorial work at *Sinister Wisdom*: preserving our lesbian past ignites lesbian futures, particularly when that work is done intergenerationally. In *Sinister Wisdom* 123: *Tribute to* Conditions, a panoply of voices reflect on *Conditions*, from women involved in producing the journal to women encountering the journal for the first time through the work of curating this issue. Many resonances between the past and the present combine in this issue; collectively they call us into a more vibrant, more vital lesbian future. I hope you enjoy reading!

Although I am writing this note during the summer of 2021, when you read it, the fall fundraising campaign will be complete and so I want to thank everyone for giving generously to support the work of *Sinister Wisdom*. Over the past year we have seen extraordinary growth for *Sinister Wisdom*. Our readership is expanding, our presence in the world grows with new online events, writing workshops, and other spaces, and our commitment to nurturing lesbian literature and arts continues to swell. Thank you to everyone for making this possible.

Here is one truth: I cherish my collection of *Conditions*, all seventeen issues produced by a hardy, committed collection of lesbian-feminists in the 1970s and 1980s. I treasure this work done with Cheryl and Shromona to create this tribute to *Conditions*. I also imagine that even greater things are in store for our collective lesbian future. Join me in the powerful recollections of what once was and in the wild imaginings of what will be.

In sisterhood,

Julie

Julie R Enszer, PhD
Editor and Publisher, *Sinister Wisdom*
January 2022

NOTES FOR A SPECIAL ISSUE

It tasted like the knowledge we have from birth: that we must suck—mouth to the body of another—or we die.
—Carmen Maria Machado, "The Mourners" (2020)

No fires immediately threatening us. Still I am keeping the car packed just in case.
—Dorothy Allison, personal correspondence (2020)

For this special issue, we have reached back forty-three years to the beginnings of *Conditions*, "a [feminist] magazine of writing for women with an emphasis on writing by lesbians," founded by Elly Bulkin, Jan Clausen, Irena Klepfisz, and Rima Shore in 1977, a year later than the founding of *Sinister Wisdom*. So, we feel it fitting that *Sinister Wisdom* should produce this special issue to honor one of the signal publications of the late Women in Print Movement, a time of prodigious writing, organizing, and creating when women "seized the time" and the means for our own revolution in letters. This special issue pays tribute to *Conditions* as one of a number of US feminist publications that asserted, in the words of Jaime Harker and Cecilia Konchar Farr, for thirteen years that "books could be revolutionary, that language could remake the world, and that writing mattered in a profound way."

To help us effect this tribute to a publication whose first issue was produced forty-four years ago, we invited the four founding editors—Elly Bulkin, Irena Klepfisz, Jan Clausen, and Rima Shore—and all members of the eleven editorial collectives to write their reflections. Jan and Rima wrote marvelous essays about their work for *Conditions*. Irena graciously granted an interview with Julie R. Enszer and Shromona Mandal, which Shromona transcribed. Though she could not at the time of publication write a reflection, Elly generously contributed from her archive letters, flyers, photographs, and many other ephemera. The co-editors are deeply grateful to Elly for her gift. We also invited Barbara Smith, as guest co-editor of *Conditions: Five / The Black Women's Issue*, to provide a reflection, to which she happily agreed. *Conditions: Five / The Black Women's Issue* had such a profound influence on Black feminist writing and theorizing, African American studies, women's studies, and humanities across the board. We almost forget its impact. Without it, there would have been no *Home Girls: A Black Feminist Anthology*, published in 1982 and reprinted in 2000, or many other anthologies of Black women's writing—local and global.

Along with *Sinister Wisdom, Feminary, off our backs, Azalea, Common Lives/Lesbian Lives*, and so many other lesbian-feminist periodicals and publications, *Conditions* marks a point of history during which lesbians produced our literature and ourselves as progressive, radical, and revolutionary women *in print*—and *in the streets*—practicing an intersectional politics (as you will witness from Elly's photos included here). Barbara Smith, often a contributor to *Conditions*, offers a personal-historical reflection of events that culminated in the special issue, and summarizes her experience:

> [The *Conditions* collective] did not shy away from looking at the consequences of the intertwined oppressions of race, class, gender, and sexuality and unlike many feminist and lesbian publications, they wanted the magazine to reflect those challenging political realities.

Dorothy Allison (editorial collective member, 1981–85) telegraphs the perils of everyday life and everyday sexuality in the San Francisco Bay Area and gives us her ponderously anxious reflection in real today time: "No fires immediately threatening us. Still I am keeping the car packed just in case." Poet Cheryl Clarke (1981–90) recounts the rigors of running an independent publication in New York City/Brooklyn. Founding editors Rima Shore (1976–82) and Jan Clausen (1976–82) contribute two remembrances in luscious prose of their time as members of the collective and as former partners of the other two founding members. Mystery writer Randye Lordon (1985–87) gives *Conditions* credit for influencing her decision about a book contract. Audre Lorde's mentorship and legacy inspire poet Melinda Goodman's (1987–90) succinct writing in which she reflects on how Lorde's teaching inspired her to manage the intellectual and more hands-on, *sans* glamour, tasks. Mariana Romo-Carmona, with her multilingual sensibility, offers a geographic recollection of *Conditions* as a literary force that challenged the monolingual proclivity within US lesbian-feminist communities. Founding editor Irena Klepfisz (1976–80), in her interview with Julie and Shromona, remains "incredibly proud" of the important work she did to bring out the first six issues of *Conditions*.

The other part of the *Conditions* special issue pairs seventeen mixed-generation writers and artists each with one of the seventeen issues of the journal. We encouraged the writers to take whatever creative bent struck their queer forms and fanc/fantas/ies. And they did. So this section is a medley of autobiography, theorizing, fiction-writing, poetry-writing, criticism, and straight-up essay addressing Issues *One* through *Seventeen*.

Rachel Corbman is first with her assessment of *Conditions: One* as a model for creating, in the words of one of its contributors, "livable worlds in writing." Shawn(ta) Smith Cruz gives us a lushly autobiographical rendering through the lens of *Conditions: Two.* And her image of the "shopping-bag lady," as she muses on Irena Klepfisz's unforgettable "Women Without Children/Women Without Families/Women Alone," is finally wrenching. Sarah Schulman's thoughtful and testy essay on *Conditions: Three* advises us that these pages will have to be "harvested, taught, valued" if lesbian-feminist culture is to be accurately portrayed. Andrea Canaan's lovely and wistful writing on *Conditions: Four* says the best about our periodicals—that they bolster our commitments to being out and activist lesbians, doing our work. Cheryl Hopson's tribute to *Conditions: Six* is an amazingly versed homage to an issue that is often called the fiction issue and is one of *Conditions'* most voluminous. Amy Haejung, in meditating on *Conditions: Seven*, draws her fictionalized reflection from some of the Latina, Native American, and Asian writers published therein: i.e., Rocky Gámez, Paula Gunn Allen, and Nellie Wong. "I was . . . privileged enough to see the quarantine induced by the pandemic that gobbled up this year of our lives as an opportunity to transform, to heal, to reckon, to pause, to familiarize myself with myself," Carmen Rios pronounces as she offers her examination of *Conditions: Eight* (1982). SaraEllen Strongman has the unenviable task of responding to *Conditions: Nine* (1983). (Cheryl notes, I am biased here, because I was deeply involved in the development of this particular issue.) However, Strongman is equal to the task of calling out "the anxieties" of the magazine, of feminist publishing, and "of the broader feminist movement." In their responses to Issues *Five* (1979) and *Ten* (1984), Mecca Jamilah Sullivan and Shromona Mandal, respectively, experiment with provocative futurist fictions. Barrie Jean Borich pegs her reflection on *Conditions: Eleven/Twelve /The Double Issue* (1985) to her own development first as a lesbian and then as a "queer femme," and states that *Conditions* laid the "groundwork" for "the kind of writing we still *need* to theorize the place of all our bodies in history" (ital mine). Rachel Afi Quinn is made to recall her coming-of-age and coming to name herself as a West African (Ghanaian) queer in diaspora as she considers *Conditions: Thirteen / International Focus I* (1986) and her "kinship" to Ghanaian poet Abena Busia's "Achimota." Adriana María Garriga-López recognizes her young queer and Puerto Rican self in *Conditions: Fourteen / International Focus II* (1987), and plunges it deeply in the interstices of global and local. "The Mourners," Carmen Maria Machado's lyrical remembrance of *Conditions: Fifteen* (1988), pays especial tribute to Sapphire's "Eat," Deborah

Salazar's "They Were Sobbing," and Pamela Sneed's "Rapunzel." Like a greatest-hits R&B LP, *Conditions: Sixteen / A Retrospective* (1989), with exquisite cover art by Eve Sandler, is spun with measured eloquence by scholar, *Sinister Wisdom* board member, and activist Red Washburn. Naomi Extra takes on *Conditions: Seventeen* and maximizes the end with thoughtful and cogent commentary on lesbian and queer thought in the issue.

Thirty-nine years ago, Carroll Oliver (1981–83) made a memorable impression on the *Conditions* editorial collective with her intellect, her youth, and her energy. We have devoted a section of this issue to Carroll, who died of AIDS in 1992. Her good friend Akasha (Gloria) Hull, also a *Conditions* contributor (Issues *One*, *Four*, *Five*), offers an elegant memory of Carroll. Collective member Jan Clausen remembers Carroll's youth and mystery. And Cheryl, also a sister-collective member, wrote our memorial tribute. The co-editors would like to thank her cousin, the visual artist Kevin Sampson, for his willingness to give us print information, photos of Carroll and her mother—Vernell Carroll, who died in 2012—and other information.

Sinister Wisdom 116: *Making Connections*, by heralding the "rich stories of bookstores and publications . . . [that] served as important ways women made connections" through myriad newsletters, newspapers, and stapled-together manuals and manifestos from ditto and mimeograph copiers (Enszer, "Notes for a Magazine," Sinister Wisdom 116 (2020), 6), rather sets the stage for our *Sinister Wisdom* 123: *A Tribute to Conditions*. Crucial telegraphs. *Conditions* epitomizes a generation of independent lesbian-feminist publishing—just before printing was given over to word-processing and the desktop computer (about which we are all ecstatic)—when we still did layout with copy, paste, and graph paper, as you will hear from editors Jan Clausen and Jewelle Gomez.

For Cheryl, this issue has been a joy to co-edit because it allows her to pay a long-overdue tribute to the publication and people— past and present—who changed her dull life. Julie Enszer's life hasn't been dull since she took over the editorship of *Sinister Wisdom* and learned what it is to edit a publication for lesbians, who are not always the easiest audience to satisfy. Never have been. I know a little something about lesbian audiences. Shromona Mandal's life has become more interesting (not that much) since she teamed up with Julie (and then Cheryl teamed up with both of them to co-edit this tribute issue); Shromona has since agreed to join the Sinister Wisdom Board. Welcome, young sister.

So, finally, we are happy to offer this issue to *Sinister Wisdom* readers, who once might also have been *Conditions* readers, but also to celebrate a period (1977–90) of lesbian print and publishing history. *Sinister Wisdom* understands the vital importance of promulgating the lesbian literary good news, and that *Conditions: a feminist magazine of writing with an emphasis on writing by lesbians* was one of our most marvelous, radical beacons. And the lesbian literary good news continues.

See all seventeen issues of Conditions digitized at the Lesbian Poetry Archive: http://www.lesbianpoetryarchive.org/conditions

Cheryl Clarke, Julie R. Enszer, Shromona Mandal, Co-Editors
Winter 2022

A N N O U N C I N G   C o n d i t i o n s

       Conditions is a new magazine of women's writing with an emphasis on writing by lesbians, which will appear three times per year and will be distributed nationally. It will reflect women's perceptions of themselves, each other, of the conditions of their lives, and the world around them.

       We are interested in receiving manuscripts of POETRY, SHORT FICTION, NOVEL excerpts, DRAMA, and other creative forms (JOURNAL entries, excerpts from CORRESPONDENCE, TRANSLATIONS, etc.).

       We are also interested in receiving CRITICAL ARTICLES on conflicts and changes in the women's/lesbian movements; women's institutions such as collectives and presses; issues involving race, class, age; problems of lesbian relationships--money, children, parents; and other topics we hope you'll suggest.

       We welcome REVIEWS and review copies. We are especially committed to publicizing and reviewing women's press publications.

       We are concerned that women's/lesbian publications have often failed to reflect the experiences and viewpoints of Third World, working-class, and older women. We want Conditions to include work in a variety of styles by both published and unpublished writers of many different backgrounds. We welcome submissions from all women, lesbian or not, who feel that a commitment to other women is an integral part of their lives.

       Please send manuscripts to:

> Conditions
> 610 Sixth Street
> Brooklyn, New York 11215

Only manuscripts accompanied by a stamped self-addressed envelope will be returned. The deadline for the winter issue is November 1, 1976.

T H E   E D I T O R S   O F   C o n d i t i o n s

       We are four friends. We are lesbian-feminists who are poets, writers, editors, reviewers. We have been involved in small press publishing (layout, publicity, national distribution), readings, feminist conferences, and writing workshops.

       ELLY BULKIN is co-editor of *Amazon Poetry: An Anthology* of lesbian poetry (Out & Out Books), and works at the Women's Center of Brooklyn College. *JAN CLAUSEN* is the author of a book of poetry, *After Touch* (Out & Out Books), and "The Politics of Publishing and the Lesbian Community" (*Sinister Wisdom*, November issue). *IRENA KLEPFISZ* is the author of a book of poetry, *periods of stress* (Out & Out Books). *RIMA SHORE* is studying Russian literature, and has reviewed books regularly in the *Chicago Sun-Times*.

REFLECTIONS
ON
CONDITIONS

FOUNDING CORRESPONDENCE
Saved by Elly Bulkin

D ear Jan & Elly—   June 27, 1976

First, Jan, I'm awfully glad you're asking these questions, glad for the same reason you're asking them—that I'll be forced to rethink these issues. Right now I'm working on the *Sinister Wisdom* editorial on whatever it is—Harriet and Catherine asked me to write about my past two years. I think it's partly therapy they have in mind—and it's effective. The writing-out of what troubles, depresses, angers, confuses, frightens me helps to order the confusion and lower the level of pain. Well, this is just a little digression on the value of being asked questions that require some analysis.

Also, Jan, I enjoy your pictures—like the shaven head chasing you all down the stairs—and your view on separatist and commercial publications. Don't stop writing me those good letters—and I promise both of you I'll rally (Remember, Elly, how I used to answer your letters the same day always—one spring, a long time ago last year?) A lot of things have taken their toll this year but I'm not going to be unsettled and uncertain forever or even much longer now. Don't give up on me and don't stop writing.

Have y'all spoken with Joan Larkin. In early June I told her a whole lot about my anger with the so-called "feminist" publications and more recently about my decision to do a focus with *Margins* (probably only part of an issue), but I haven't heard from her. At any rate, I will run the review of Out and Out books in both *SW* and *Margins*. But I told you that, Elly, already.

Elly, would you be poetry editor for *Sinister Wisdom?* Before I came to Florida I visited the *Sinister Wisdom* women in Charlotte. They told me they were looking for a poetry editor and of course

I thought of you. They agreed you would be the perfect poetry editor and I told them I would ask you. So . . . I <u>do</u> respect these women and I think *Sinister Wisdom* will fast become a publication you'll be proud to be associated with. (Shit, Elly, Adrienne Rich sent them $50)—what more endorsement?)

Anyway, will you think it over? I thought 1) you'd enjoy editing poetry 2) *Sinister Wisdom* will become a significant l/f[1] vehicle (I don't think I'm mistaken (of course) that Harriet and Catherine[2] are more intelligent and have better aesthetic judgement (they <u>do</u> have more training and more years of living—Harriet is trained as a philosopher and she is a poet in her soul. I think and Catherine has a degree in English and she's a director and playwright and is mid-'50s) than Gina and (Laurel.[3])) And that it's a publication (like *AQ*) which will earn its reputation and you will be pleased to be a part of it.

June 28 I was so tired last night when I quit this [arrow pointing up to the letter]—I'm surprised it's as coherent as it is. Anyway, Elly, it's an invitation to be poetry editor of *Sinister Wisdom*. I hope you'll accept.

Take care, friends, and I'll see you in fall sometime.

Love, Beth[4]

---

1 An abbreviation for lesbian/feminist

2 Harriet Desmoines and Catherine Nicholson, the founders of *Sinister Wisdom*.

3 Gina Corvina and Laurel Galana, the editors and publishers of *Amazon Quarterly*. For some issues of this influential magazine, visit http://www.lesbianpoetryarchive.org/AmazonQuarterly.

4 Beth Hodges, editor of the second issue of *Sinister Wisdom*, a special issue focused on Lesbian Writing and Publishing. The issue is available as a PDF here: http://www.sinisterwisdom.org/sites/default/files/Sinister%20Wisdom%202.pdf.

610 6 Street
Brooklyn, NY 11215
July 4, [1976][5]

D ear Harriet and Catherine,
    I was delighted to hear from Beth that you were interested in my becoming poetry editor of *Sinister Wisdom*. I also found that I had all sorts of questions I wanted to communicate with you about before making a firm commitment.

Many of my questions are very basic, attempts, I think, to compensate for the fact that I find myself considering an offer to work on a magazine I've never seen, put out by 2 women I've never met. Why did you decide to start it? How much will it be? How long will it be? How many pages per issue do you plan to devote to poetry? What other kind of material will it contain? Fiction? Reviews? Critical articles? Graphics? Do you see it having a specific thematic emphasis and/or political perspective? Is there material that, because of topic, point of view and/or author you'd consider inappropriate to appear in *SW*?

How would you see my role as poetry editor—as (space permitting) making final decisions about what to use, as a consultant subject to your final approval? Might you be selecting a specific theme for an entire issue that you'd want compatible poetry for? Would you want me to do short reviews of new lesbian poetry books?

I'm looking forward to hearing from you and to finding out if you want to know additional things about me? I feel that the dedication and Prefatory Note to *Amazon Poetry*[6] accurately states

---

5 This letter is dated the day of the release of the first issue of *Sinister Wisdom*.

6 These pages from *Amazon Poetry* are available at the Lesbian Poetry Archive, http://www.lesbianpoetryarchive.org/AmazonPoetry

the personal/political perspective that determines the specifics of my life and should be the starting point in your decision as to whether you want me to work with you on this project.

In sisterhood,
[Elly Bulkin]

30 July 76

Dear Elly Bulkin,

You have every reason in the world to be irritated at Catherine & me because we've bumbled badly. The last time Beth was here (while *Sinister Wisdom* was at the printer's), we talked about wanting a poetry editor, since neither Catherine nor I feel at all competent to winnow these poetry submissions. We couldn't imagine who would want to do it and who we would trust to do it. Beth mentioned you, and our immediate response was "wonder, but she wouldn't do it, and besides how can we ask her?" So Beth said she would ask you.

But now Beth is still in Florida, and I don't think she's seen her Georgia mailbox in weeks. We drove down to Jacksonville two weeks ago (on a Southern distribution/pleasure trip—it was hot as hell) and talked with her. She thought maybe you'd replied to her letter, but we agreed that how could you say yes or no or even maybe until you'd heard from us and seen the magazine. So we were to write to you as soon as we returned to Charlotte. Well, we're in Charlotte now and finally confident enough to ask but feeling like raving assholes for having waited so long.

The magazine is enclosed. If the vision tempts you and you might be interested in doing the poetry, please let us know. And again, we apologize for the bumbling.

In sister struggle,
Harriet Desmoines
3115 Country Club Drive Charlotte NC 28205[7]

---

7 This address is handwritten at the bottom of the page.

30 July 76

Dear Elly,

Amazon Poetry arrived yesterday, and we thank you very much. It more than satisfied our expectations. The statement at the beginning is fine with us, and the selection of poems is marvelous.

So, here is what we would like: for you to take full control over a maximum of 15 pages per issue. (15 pages 6" x 9"[8] would be between []& [] of the size issue we're projecting—in other words, the rest of the issues will be fatter than the first.) We would not want to exercise any veto over what you had chosen, so you could just regard the poetry pages as yours, to experiment with as you pleased. You could include reviews or not, center your pages around a theme or not, etc.

We don't think there'll be any particular problems with your living in New York City and the journal coming out of Charlotte. If you decide to do it, the first issue you'd be responsible for would be March '77. The submission deadline for that issue is December 15, 1976. You'd need to get your pages to us by January 15, 1977. There's supposed to be a unifying theme for the prose in that issue, "A Sinister View of Humanism," but obviously you wouldn't need to pay any attention to that when selecting the poetry. You would have to trust our final judgment on the layout, though we'd follow your suggestions as much as we could.

If all this sounds agreeable to you, please let us know.

---

8 The dimensions are handwritten in the letter margin with an arrow.

The one radical bookstore in Charlotte that we're sure would've carried *Amazon Poetry* is now defunct, but the people involved are setting up a mail order distribution—and we'll get *A.P.* into their catalogue. We'll also check the remaining possibilities in town and let you know. What are your bulk rates? And do you have suggestions on which places (bookstores, etc.) in NYC we should contact about distributing *SW?*

Harriet[9]
3116 Country Club Drive Charlotte NC 28205[10]

---

9   A handwritten signature.

10   Also handwritten at the bottom of the page.

610 6 Street
Brooklyn, NY 11215
August 6, 1976

Dear Harriet,

Thanks very much for the first issue of *Sinister Wisdom*, which I was finally able to retrieve (unforwarded) from my old apartment house. I was excited to see a new magazine that would provide a needed outlet for lesbian writing.

My delay in writing stems, I think, from my own ambivalence about working on *SW*. The offer to have 15 pages to do with as I like is of course very appealing; my immediate response was to think of poets I'd contact to fill them. I did, however, have some difficulties with the magazine's overall vision—with a stress on lesbian imagination/consciousness that seems to me to lead to many selections that are inner-focused, abstract, sometimes, allegorical, unconnected to what for me is a reality much more grounded in concrete oppressions/struggles.

Living in New York City where the women's and lesbian movements are sufficiently segmented that it is often difficult to remember that they are supposed to be "communities," I feel some discomfort at the absence of the concept/theme of struggle between women, [crossed out] with the repeated emphasis on the need to "join our hands together in strength and in love, the radiant power of women." Although I do see women as the source of my strength and love, I also see them as a source of a good deal of my anger and disappointment, perhaps because on some level I expect more of them/us.

My first impulse was to put aside my reservations and accept a job as a poetry editor that I would very much like—on a magazine that I hope will grow and reach many women. But finally it seemed dishonest for me to accept a job in which I would be putting together poetry and poetry reviews that I would see as reflecting a vision that differs from yours. If we lived near each other and could communicate more immediately than by letter, I would be able to get a sense of both of you and your expectations for *SW*, then I would have a far clearer sense of the precise nature of our differences and the extent to which they allow for a working relationship.

Thinking and talking about my feeling about these issues over the past week has made me keenly aware of my own need for personal access to women I work with so that we can share our feelings/thoughts more easily; and for the sense that the aspect of a magazine that I take responsibility for be a thoroughly integrated part of the whole. A result has been to re-raise the possibility of my doing a magazine with some friends here, something we've been toying with for about a year, but have never been able to commit ourselves to. Although all of the women I'd be working with do not share my political perspective (a combination, I think, of a socialism-feminism and lesbian-feminism, sometimes more of the form[er], sometimes more of the latter), I feel that because we all live in Brooklyn we could struggle things out to produce a magazine that would reflect in its entirety, the perspectives that we do share.

Many thanks for your offer to me. I hope you'll be soon through the hard initial stage of trying to distribute nationally, a magazine that is still an unknown quantity to the bookstores you're contacting. In New York, you should write to the two women's bookstores: Labyris, 33 Barrow St, NY, NY and Womanbooks, 281 West 92 St., NY, NY. Labyris is small and not always very well organized, but Womanbooks carries an impressively large stock and I'm quite sure will be interested in carrying *SW*. A third possibility is the Oscar Wilde Bookstore (can't find the address but will send it along when I do), which carries lots of lesbian (and gay male) literature. It's owned by a man. In any event, it was, to my knowledge, the only NYC bookstore that carried the lesbian issues of *Margins* and, if you wanted to distribute through it, would be very likely carry *SW*. Let me know if I can help you with further information about distributing around here.

For our books we charge 60/40 to bookstores (we get $1.20 for *Amazon Poetry*) plus postage; usually we bill bookstores rather than get prepaid.

I understand that you and Catherine will be doing a panel at the MLA in December and am very much looking forward to meeting you there.[11]

In sisterhood,
[Elly Bulkin]

Elly Bulkin, a founding editor of *Conditions* and *Bridges: A Journal for Jewish Feminists and Our Friends*, edited *Lesbian Fiction: An Anthology*; co-edited, with Joan Larkin, *Amazon Poetry* and *Lesbian Poetry*; and co-authored, with Minnie Bruce Pratt and Barbara Smith, *Yours in Struggle: Three Feminist Perspectives on Anti-Semitism and Racism*. Her articles include "Racism and Writing: Some Implications for White Lesbian Critics" (*Sinister Wisdom* 13) and "Jews, Blacks, and Lesbian Teens in the 1940s: Jo Sinclair's *The Changelings* and 'The Long Moment'" (2016). An activist since the 1970s, Elly has worked with such groups as DARE (Dykes Against Racism Everywhere), Women Free Women in Prison, Feminist Action Network, New Jewish Agenda's National Feminist Task Force, JVP's Network Against Islamophobia, Jews Against Anti-Muslim Racism, and SONG (Southerners on New Ground).

---

11 The Modern Languages Association met in New York City in December 1976.

FALLING IN LOVE WITH PUBLISHING: AN INTERVIEW

Irena Klepfisz

Irena Klepfisz is one of the four founders of *Conditions*. In addition, she is a distinguished poet, scholar, activist, and Yiddish translator. Klepfisz was a member of the *Conditions* editorial collective from 1976 until 1981. Julie R. Enszer and Shromona Mandal interviewed Klepfisz on May 13, 2020 via Zoom for this issue of *Sinister Wisdom*. The edited transcript of the interview is below.

Julie R. Enszer (JRE): Tell us about your experience with *Conditions*.

Irena Klepfisz (IK): I've always been incredibly proud of my association with *Conditions*. I got involved in the groundwork for it and worked on the first six issues, which took four years [to publish]—we weren't able to do it any faster. But in that time *Conditions*' reputation just grew.

The most exciting aspect [of *Conditions*] was discovering and giving space to as yet unknown writers. We wanted the magazine to draw from and answer to the needs of readers and writers outside of the mainstream. And yet, oddly, the first few issues were almost guaranteed to move us if not into, at least in proximity to the mainstream. I'll get to that later. Eventually we published work by writers like Alice Walker, Audre Lorde, Blanche Cook, Marilyn Hacker, and many others connected primarily with mainstream journals and presses. I think the fact that these writers wanted to place their work in *Conditions* gave it a kind of literary and political legitimacy—maybe respectability. Looking back, it looks pretty amazing and heady. But at the time it felt pretty grungy [laughs]. It was really hard. During that time we did six issues in four years and the four of us only edited five of them. I think *Conditions: Six* was in the fourth year.

JRE: How did you become involved?

IK: Let me describe the road and encounters that led me to *Conditions.*

I came out in '73 when I was thirty-two. I'd lost my job at LIU (Long Island University). I was very confused about everything: How to earn a living? Was I with men? Was I with women? I decided to collect unemployment and fulfill a lifelong fantasy of writing poetry by the ocean. I learned to drive and rented a tiny house in Montauk. The summer before I was to return to the city to do I-don't-know-what, I bumped into an old friend, a dyke with whom I'd been in group therapy. She connected me with a dyke who lived in East Hampton, Blanche Wiesen Cook, and her partner Clare Coss and their friend Alice Kessler-Harris (in 1974, all three public reputations for these women were still in the future). We met at an East Hampton lesbian bar, Patchez (Pat was the owner). "Rock the Boat" was *the* song of that summer, and on weekends like 50 million dykes danced and sang there. It became home.

At some point I probably said something about poetry, and Blanche said, "Oh, when you get back to the city, contact Joan Larkin; she's forming a lesbian writing support group." I did. One of its members was Jan Clausen. The group did a couple of public readings and advertised itself as Seven Women Poets. We were all dykes. I don't remember the rationale for not using the L word. At this time, Jan was already with Elly, and they and Joan and I started to talk about a possible joint project, a press—Out & Out Books—that would serve as an imprint for three self-published poetry books (Joan, Jan, me) and an anthology of lesbian poetry (Elly). And that's what we did.

Rima and I were hanging out somewhat with Jan and Elly. And it was a bit like Judy Garland saying, "Oh, let's put on a show!" You know: fools rush in where angels fear to tread. Somebody said, "We should have a magazine!" That's really how it started as I remember it. (My memory's been jogged and I do recall there was discussion about Elly doing a poetry section for *SW*. It still was a big leap from thinking about a column or section to a whole magazine.) Both Jan and I felt limited in available outlets for our work. So the idea of a magazine was in part an expression of our personal needs (as was Out & Out Books) and in part a recognition of the needs of both readers and writers "out there." It took a lot of discussion to come up with that byline: "A magazine of women's writing with an emphasis on writing by lesbians." We were frequently (mis) perceived as a lesbian magazine because we were all dykes. But we had a conscious commitment to writing by all women of color and working-class women. We didn't want to preclude these women by making *Conditions* exclusively for lesbians. We recognized the political implications of a literary endeavor.

JRE: Can you talk a bit more about the lesbian component?

IK: We were committed to the lesbian "cause," so to speak, but none of us would have described ourselves as "lesbian separatists," i.e., as lesbians working exclusively with and for other lesbians. In the late '70s there were a lot of tensions around that term and around women who identified themselves as such. I recall my first meeting with Elana Dykewomon, today one of my dearest, closest friends. She had invited us Out & Out women to read in Lesbian Gardens (lesbians only) in Northampton, Massachusetts. This was still pre-*Conditions*, I think. When we arrived, a bitter argument erupted over a straight woman who had come into the space under false pretenses, and they wanted to eject her. In the end, we didn't read and left. . . It was a very fractious time.

As always, there were contradictions. I would never have described myself as a lesbian separatist, though for many years my personal life, in practice, included lesbians only. But my politics and theoretical grounding were never exclusively lesbian. At the same time, I should add that I feel my "career" is indebted entirely to lesbians. Lesbians were the ones who made possible my becoming known as a writer; it was lesbians who accepted me and embraced my work before the Jewish and Yiddishist communities. And that started, of course, with Seven Women Poets, Out & Out Books, and *Conditions*.

At *Conditions* we were always conscious of homophobia both inside and outside the mainstream feminist movement and believed it had to be addressed. Sometimes it was quite subtle. For example, I remember we were stunned to find out (don't remember exactly how) that the *Women's Review of Books* would never place a book on its front page—visible when mailed— that had the word "lesbian" in its title or in its review's opening paragraphs. That meant that books like Elly's *Lesbian Poetry* were automatically excluded from being featured. Why? We heard it was to protect closeted subscribers. A brown wrapper would have solved the problem. I'm not sure when the *WRB* resolved this issue. But that's just one example.

I know the second wave is in disrepute. I am fully aware of its limitations, some of which I personally experienced, as a lefty, a Jew, and a lesbian—much of it with straight *Jewish* "feminists" who were not modest about their homophobia among other prejudices. It was not an easy struggle. At the same time, I feel it's important to credit the movement's accomplishments—one of which was helping publicize our existence (I'll say a bit more later). As a result, *Conditions* was able to have an impact across gender, ethnic, racial, and class lines and contributed to the fight against homophobia and racism.

Specifically in terms of including lesbian content, there were complexities, such as issues of stereotypes. For example, I remember one recurring discussion was about the "miserable *Well-of-Loneliness* lesbian" whose story always ended unhappily. . . how to project a possible different ending when reality seemed so against it. We also had to deal with negative stereotypes: the lesbian alcoholic. To depict it was to enforce the stereotype; not to depict it was again to ignore reality. But what was lesbian reality? There were many.

JRE: What kind of process did you have creating the magazine?

IK: Well, when we started, we had this policy that we had to write something nice to everybody [laughs]. So we'd divide the acceptances and rejections among ourselves. But as the volume of submission increased, we inevitably had to cut back on the length of our rejection letters.

I didn't feel exactly that I had people's fate in my hands, but I did feel responsible and tried to be kind in rejections. . . and encouraging. Balancing was the discovery of something that you really liked and saying: "Oh my God, this is great. Let's use it!"

For the most part, our discussions were not difficult and were fun. But as is common in collectives, there's agreement on 98 percent of submissions, so most time is spent on the remaining 2 percent. And we'd argue, what's primary—the politics and subject or the craft and execution? Are the politics (even though the aesthetics aren't so good) so important that it should be published? Those were always the difficult discussions. I don't think they were unique to us.

JRE: The early issues of *Conditions* were so influential.

IK: I think there were a number of factors that made that happen.

First, we really stepped into it with Elly's interview with Adrienne Rich in the first two issues. That was a big way to start. Amazing. It almost guaranteed notice. At this point, Adrienne was an internationally known poet and feminist but was also emerging as an important spokesperson for lesbians and the gay movement. The interview was a very, very big deal. It enabled us to reach not only lesbians, but also the straight literary world and straight feminists.

One thing I realized recently when thinking about that time is that we—as writers and editors—made ourselves important by being associated with her. I honestly don't believe that any of us thought of it that way at the time, but looking back—we had real chutzpah. For example, in the first issue Jan contributed an essay, Rima a review, Elly the interview, and I poetry. We had put ourselves on the same platform or level as Adrienne. After the first issue, I got a personal letter from Tillie Olsen. I'm sure she saw the interview—how else? We made ourselves publicly important by association. Women started to view us and our work—as significant thinkers, creative artists, and editors—with power. Adrienne's interview in the first two issues was an enormous boost.

Equally important was Barbara Smith's essay in *Conditions: Two*, which included the second part of Adrienne's interview. Barbara was a Boston activist and a member of the Combahee River Collective. As I remember it, Elly heard her speak at an MLA meeting in NYC and asked her to contribute something to the magazine, and that something turned out to be "Toward a Black Feminist Criticism." The essay was groundbreaking and an instant classic. Again, I think the interview probably magnified Barbara's essay's visibility and reach. Her essay and the writers and the book reviews we published in subsequent issues showed that *Conditions'* commitment to women of color was not simply theoretical.

Looking back, I think we put out two very, very good issues. But I believe that both Adrienne's and Barbara's words were instrumental in giving *Conditions* legitimacy, prestige, credibility, and therefore, influence. I'm not sure how it would have fared without them.

The third factor—its importance can't be overstated—was the women's movement, the second wave, and its embrace of women writers and poets and its distribution of their work. *Conditions* was both a contributor to this movement and also its beneficiary. We contributed by being committed to small and alternative press publications, especially through our review section and promotion of other print material. And we benefited because a whole network of feminist distribution emerged over time that publicized and sold the magazine. This occurred through feminist and lesbian conferences and gatherings where we could promote our magazine, through women's bookstores that sold it, through endless feminist and lesbian journals and papers where we could advertise and promote the work of our writers, and finally through women's distribution networks. It took time, but even by the late '70s and early '80s, *Conditions* was strengthened directly and indirectly by the movement. In short, we were able to influence and reach people because we were not working in isolation. Whatever our disagreements with it and whatever its shortcomings, we were part of that national movement. And it contributed to *Conditions'* success.

JRE: What was the early vision for *Conditions*? What did the four of you talk about?

IK: We were all trying to publish the best work, but it was hard. There were issues like politics vs. art that I described before. But these also come into play when there are few options for artists and writers and space is limited. When you have too many "good" pieces you want to print, who are you going to represent? Who are you going to give space to? Who are you going to give that microphone to for those two minutes? At the end of the "final" selection—supposedly when we were finished—we would look at who and what we were planning to publish: the issues being addressed, the writers we had chosen. Did the whole reflect our political commitments and the diversity we were hoping for? Finalizing an issue was sometimes tricky.

JRE: Tell me about the reviews in *Conditions*.

IK: From the start, we knew we wanted reviews and we agreed on what we didn't want: reviews that were essentially "pans" and reviews of work that was being adequately covered elsewhere. There was no point in wasting precious space on something you didn't like—especially from a small press that most people hadn't heard of—or on books that were already well-publicized. We really wanted *Conditions* to highlight writers and presses not well-known or difficult to distribute and to give them space to be taken seriously.

And truth be told, reviews, as I remember it, were really a pain! Because we had to deal with writers who were inevitably late or inexperienced, or who didn't understand our mission. Each of us put more time into reviews than any other material in an issue. And we didn't always do so well. I don't know if you know the poetry of the late Enid Dame. She was a wonderful poet. She self-published a lot of her work. I bumped into her one time on the street in Park Slope and she started almost crying because she felt the review of her poetry was very negative. And I went back to look at it again and realized it did not have the appreciation and analysis we aimed for in a review. I empathized, but it was done. I mean, it was terrible to meet her in the street and have her that upset.

One of the big issues that we had, even with Out & Out Books, was distribution. I remember going with *Conditions: One* to the Eighth Street Bookstore in Manhattan, which had in its wonderful basement all kinds of alternative journals and magazines— probably the only mainstream bookstore that carried us from the start. But the development all around the country of women's and feminist bookstores facilitated distribution. And all the newspapers and rags— they were very important in terms of spreading the word. This was all without the internet, of course.

JRE: How did you all decide to do *Conditions: Five / The Black Women's Issue*?

IK: *Conditions: Five* seemed like the natural thing to do. We were committed to the work of women of color, but until then, all that work in *Conditions* had been judged and evaluated by four white women. It was obvious that women of color needed to be involved in that process directly and to have editorial autonomy. So we gave the complete editorial power to Lorraine Bethel and Barbara Smith. It was not a difficult decision. I don't remember the specifics of the discussions, which makes me believe that it went fairly smoothly. Toward the end, there was some tension about perceived antisemitism in one of the accepted pieces. I honestly don't remember the specifics or the resolution. Maybe the others do. But it wasn't a major conflict, or I think I would have remembered it.

Conditions: Five made the diversification of the editorial board inevitable. I suspect that my leaving the magazine may have accelerated the process, but I don't know since it started after I left. Rima and I had broken up and things became awkward and difficult. I took a leave of absence after *Conditions: Six* and then decided to leave permanently. They obviously couldn't continue with just three editors. It was hard enough with four. But I believe that even if I had stayed it would have happened because we couldn't have continued with just the four of us. We were stretched very thin. And of course if we were going to expand the editorial board it would be with women of color and working-class women.

JRE: Would you talk a little bit about your own politics at that time?

IK: It was both a difficult and exhilarating period for me. I am an immigrant and was raised in a very closed, socialist, Yiddish-speaking, Holocaust-survivors community. The focus of the first three decades of my life was the war. I really didn't know very much about American Jewish life or antisemitism or really about the US, and frankly, I was uncomfortable about being a Jew in public. My perspective was shaped by the war in Europe. I did a lot of therapy around it. So when I came out in my mid-thirties, it served as a kind of awakening, a waking up—"Irena, it's the 1970s, you're in the US" I feel that getting involved with gays and lesbians and doing *Conditions* was what enabled me to kind of get off the boat and finally land in this country.

Conditions made me think more about American history, American everything, at the same time that I was trying to figure out what I wanted for myself. I had hated graduate school but finished the PhD. And I had gotten my first full-time teaching job here in New York at LIU—which turned out to also be my last full-time teaching job. After four years, I was back doing a lot of office work and shit work. While coming out, I was also getting more involved with Jewish issues and becoming more conscious of the Yiddish culture, which I had been raised with, but which I had ignored for most of my adult life.

I found the different strains within the movement confusing. There was a big emphasis on "downward mobility," which I thought was just absurd and didn't understand. Class issues were too simplified. One woman I met, a poet, actually wept because she had to work and she would have less time for writing. I was amazed. I always knew that everyone had to work, even artists. The adults that surrounded me when I was growing up in the Bronx were all working-class—garment pieceworkers, construction workers, typesetters in printing shops (the exception was a doctor). In Poland, my mother started working at the age of twelve, after her father died. My first conscious lesson about class and capitalism occurred when a family friend, a construction worker, pointed to a building and told me: "I worked on that building. But I can't afford to live there." I was very young—around ten—but it made an impression. When I got my PhD, my mother's friends—without an invitation—gathered at her apartment and brought me flowers. We celebrated. But in the movement, I met women who were embarrassed by their PhDs, and despite my background, being somewhat intimidated, I left out the fact that I had a doctorate from my bio in my first book, *periods of stress*. Not because I thought it wasn't an important achievement, but because I thought I should be ashamed of it! Totally stupid.

I remember once having an argument with a feminist committee that was distributing scholarships. A middle-aged woman had made some kind of reference to a vacation in her application. Members argued that if she could take a vacation, then she didn't need a scholarship. They couldn't imagine poor working-class people actually managing to pull together resources for a vacation. We, of course, knew nothing about the details of this vacation—what was it exactly (certainly not a cruise), was it perhaps her first in twenty years, was it based on a trade-off (clothes, dentist). We only knew she had a vacation and was asking for financial help to attend a seminar. And God forbid this woman could take a vacation *and* participate in a seminar without totally killing herself to pay for both. I found the understanding of class really undeveloped.

So my politics had deep roots in my Jewish socialist background. At the same time, I came to realize that the Jewish activist history I'd inherited differed from what I was experiencing here in the States. About six months ago, I was on a panel about the Jewish Labor Bund's influence on my writing and work—the socialist organization that my parents had been active in before the war. I noted that unlike my parents in interwar Poland who were focused on class and anti-Semitism, my personal struggle also included homophobia—the issue that woke me up—not just in the wider society, but also in the Jewish community where I was trying to reconnect. And this was an issue that wasn't even in the vocabulary of those earlier Jewish activists in Poland.

JRE: You are one of the people who has worked to publicize the Yiddish language and Yiddish culture. You have had this protean career as a writer and editor and intellectual that has different parts that people don't see often. I'm curious how you knit this work with some of your later work?

IK: Well, *Conditions* made me fall in love with publishing. *Conditions* gave me the bug. If I could do my life over again, I would have my own publishing house. I wanted to have a *Froyen farlag*, "Women's Press" in Yiddish. I didn't intend it to be for Yiddish work only, but I wanted the press to have a Yiddish name. I love putting words and visuals on paper and sending them out into the world. A flyer, a newsletter, a memorial book, an anthology, proceedings of a conference—I love doing them all. I still love, more than anything, a physical book.

Working on *Conditions*, I acquired editorial skills and a deeper understanding of the politics of publishing, which actually mirrored much of the Jewish socialist ideology in which I was raised. Who gets seen and heard, who gets marginalized, who is disappeared. Who gets to do what they want. Who has to forget what they want and has to work. I applied this perspective to my own history and to the Yiddish culture in which I was raised. Within a couple of years after leaving *Conditions*, I began collaborating with Melanie Kaye/Kantrowitz on a Jewish women's anthology. Melanie was editing *Sinister Wisdom*, and together we physically put together *The Tribe of Dina* as a double issue of *Sinister Wisdom*. We sat in Maine for three weeks [laughs] and worked. It was just incredible. And wonderful.

Since *Conditions*, I've worked primarily on Jewish issues and most recently produced memorial books for the 120th anniversary of the founding of the Jewish Labor Bund and the 75th anniversary of the Warsaw Ghetto Uprising. It's ironic that my experiences in the late '70s were partly responsible for my ability to return to the subjects and culture which I had such difficulty integrating into my life when I first started editing *Conditions*.

I've always wanted there to be a written record of events and ideas that move me. I've had two primary obsessions or passions. One was working with women (many, many lesbians) on the Israel-Palestine conflict. So many of us put enormous energy into that work. But it's turned out to be a terrible, painful failure. My other passion has been the promotion of Yiddish women writers and intellectuals—that's been more successful. I'm proud of raising awareness of the marginalization of women in Yiddish culture and seeing their subsequent inclusion. Today in Jewish studies, every other person is translating Yiddish women writers, but in 1982–83—when Melanie and I began working on *The Tribe of Dina*—nobody was even thinking about this issue and mocked those who raised it.

My students often say when they're concerned about addressing an issue: "Oh! You know, there's only two or three of us, and we're so small." And I tell them: "Just start it!" I think about *Conditions*, or Kitchen Table Press, and I think about Gloria Anzaldúa's thousands upon thousands of copies of *Borderlands* and that it's required reading in English and women's studies courses. And that was made possible by a bunch of women just sitting around a kitchen table or hanging out and someone saying: "Let's do a magazine!" or "Let's start a press!" And they got it done. Without the internet.

It's very defeating to project too far ahead: "Oh, we're not going to reach anybody." Do what you need to do! You have three people? Work with three people. *Conditions* wasn't ever that big when you compare it to the *Paris Review* or the *New York Review of Books*. I think we began with a run of 1,000 copies and moved at some point to 2,500. Only *Conditions: Five* was a big seller and was reprinted after the first 5,000. We began printing 3,000 with *Conditions: Six* because it was a primarily fiction issue and we thought it would be popular. So *Conditions* was never huge. I mean, there are those twenty-three boxes that you told me about. Still, the influence was enormous. The Jewish Labor Bund was founded in 1897 with twelve people in a Vilna attic. And by the 1930s, it was a Jewish mass movement across Europe! In 2013 three Black women started Black Lives Matter. Three!

So, you can start small. You don't need to start with a hundred people. In fact, you probably can't even get off the ground with a hundred people. With three people or four people, you can do it. And you can change people's lives.

MATERIAL CONDITIONS

Jan Clausen

In what follows, I have often found myself saying "we," as though channeling the undivided perspective of all four founding editors of Conditions. *Given significant differences in our views that sometimes turned editorial meetings into tense "struggle sessions," this is clearly problematic, yet to speak purely as an individual also feels false: producing the magazine was an intensely dialogic process.* Conditions *began in conversations between two couples, those four-way exchanges already deeply marked by what each pair of lovers had been saying to each other in private about feminist movement and lesbian literature. In Elly's and my case, because our early relationship developed in tandem with the magazine's founding, it becomes even more difficult for me to distinguish her thinking from my own. Notwithstanding which, my resort to collective pronouns should be read as a device bordering on fiction.*

From my email to Julie Enszer agreeing to write this piece:

I "hung fire" in replying, as Henry James would say, because I wondered what I would write about the magazine that would be celebratory enough yet honest enough. Not that I have any doubts about the worth of [*Conditions*] or the "not me, us" that it represented—just that the connections among all the "me's" making that "us" were often so difficult. Which, in a way, is exactly the thing that needs to be portrayed in order to be really useful to anyone now or in the future. This morning, though, it struck me—I could approach it from the angle of the material *conditions* that attended the birth of the magazine, everything from how the co-founders knew each other . . . to how we survived while putting out a periodical that cost money and paid no one, to what it was like to stuff envelopes and make corrections to camera-ready copy on a light table. I think that might be of some use!

When I wrote these words, I was thinking of how much has changed in the socioeconomic and technological landscape since 1977, when *Conditions: One* appeared. I hoped that a look at the nitty-gritty details of putting together a collectively run, lesbian-centered, feminist "little magazine" in the analog era might be helpful to anyone plotting their own cultural insurrection in a desperate time of quickening radical ferment. Only later did I grasp the obvious: how my proposed focus echoed the passion, shared by the co-founders and many contributors, to expose the material pressures that constrain women's lives in relation to the creativity of our art and organizing.

Our choice of name for the magazine, initially inspired by a persona poem of Irena's, delighted us with its breadth of connotation; the plural emphasis captured our view of lesbian lives as defined by an almost infinite range of specific circumstances, many of which had yet to be described. "Conditions" often presented as barriers, but might be turned around—reimagined as precursors of liberation. Yet imagination would fail without critical awareness. In order to shape a feminist future, we needed to face the limitations and divisions baked into our everyday realities.

In other words, we editors rejected the rosy view of some lesbian separatists and so-called cultural feminists who claimed that the main prerequisite to building an autonomous, nurturing, woman-centered reality was successful exorcism of "the prick in our heads." By invoking "conditions," we invoked the relevance of power configurations in the society at large, as these were reproduced in feminist spaces in ways that not only blocked personal liberation but threatened to keep our movements divided and weak. The situation called for a layered scrutiny of everything, from large structural factors to the ways women dealt with each other in meetings, in bars, in the workplace, in bed, in literature.

This concern to foreground the concrete dimensions of our lives, alongside our theories and imaginative products, is striking across contributors and issues. "The whole issue of homophobia in women, not just 'out there' in the patriarchal world, has got to be confronted and talked about, dealt with as the real problem," Adrienne Rich, interviewed by Elly, declares in *Conditions: One* (56). "Thematically, stylistically, aesthetically and conceptually Black women writers manifest common approaches to the act of creating literature as a direct result of the specific political, social and economic experience they have been obliged to share," Barbara Smith asserts in "Toward a Black Feminist Criticism" (*Conditions: Two*, 32). In Irena's short story "The Journal of Rachel Robotnik," published in *Conditions: Six*, the protagonist keeps a journal detailing the gap between the aesthetic satisfactions of her writing and the daily grind of her job as a medical transcriber. Suspecting that her boss might be planning to lay her off, she notes: "Was excited for abt 30 sec—then filled w/ complete, utter panic. To go on unemployment w/ no savings of any sort. I've been thru that—the constant hustling—on the books, off the books. Always trying to be 1 step ahead, at least 1 month's rent ahead. Constantly at the mercy of the phone, unable to turn down any shit job that comes along because there's never any guarantee there'll be another one later. So ultimately the writing came last anyway" (138). In *Conditions: Seven*, Cherríe Moraga frames her review of *Top Ranking: A Collection of Articles on Racism and Classism in the Lesbian Community* with a resonant comment by "una compañera": "We must know how a lesbian life relates to the context of all life" (140). Plumbing the contradictions of "the politics of identity" in "Sisterhood—And My Brothers" (*Conditions: Eight*), Rima asks, "Do I seek to identify with Jews in the abstract, but not with the brothers I have loved all my life?" (98–99).

I recall the atmosphere of our early collective meetings as a curious blend of sober skepticism and irrational, if crucially buoying, exuberance. We would do what had never been done. We would help make a space—one space among many—where lesbians and other feminists could grasp the core truths of our lives and our relationships to others. I think it's fair to say that Elly and I, at least, saw no meaningful wall or border between literary expression—poems, stories, creative nonfiction, plays—and the magazine's discursive and more activist-oriented content. *Conditions* began at the crest of what I would later refer to as "a [feminist] movement of poets,"[1] and though my essay of that title reflects dampened enthusiasm for poetry as a political tool, in the mid-seventies I had yet to acknowledge significant tension between fodder for organizing and what worked for me as art.

Under the circumstances, differences over the place of literary standards in our editorial process sparked some of the collective's fiercest debates—yet the four of us broadly agreed on our goal of reflecting "women's perceptions of themselves, each other, the conditions of their lives, and of the world around them" (from an editors' note included in the first seven issues). Given this ambitious program, what were our own realities? What concrete circumstances, helpful and not, surrounded *Conditions'* founding?

At the time we began to talk of starting a magazine, three of the editors had already collaborated on other feminist literary projects. Irena and I had met through Seven Women Poets, a Brooklyn-based poetry support group. In 1975, we cooperatively published first poetry collections through Out & Out Books, which was also the publisher of *Amazon Poetry*, a pathbreaking lesbian anthology that Elly had edited with Joan Larkin. We were living in Park Slope in walkup apartment buildings only a few blocks apart, which greatly simplified our meeting arrangements—of

---

1 Clausen, Jan. *A Movement of Poets: Thoughts on Poetry and Feminism.* New York: Long Haul Press, 1982.

particular importance to Elly and me since we had our daughter's bedtime to consider. I was the only non-Jew and the only one of the bunch who'd recently arrived in New York, a transplant from my original home in the Pacific Northwest. Though Irena had been born in Poland during World War II and Rima hailed from the Jersey suburbs, from my perspective my co-editors were all seasoned New Yorkers, while I was the neophyte.

We four all led some version of the character Rachel Robotnik's seat-of-the-pants relationship to "the world of work," pressed by money concerns yet determined to make room for art and activism. All nominally middle-class, we were downwardly mobile in an era when that was common among radicals and artists. In any case, as vocal lesbian-feminists, we figured we'd effectively scuttled our chances at respectable careers. Coincidentally or not, we all had unsettled relationships with academia. I was the lone (and proud) college dropout. Irena and Elly had earned PhDs and briefly taught in their fields before moving on. Rima, enrolled in a doctoral program in Russian literature, would likewise take a different path after completing her degree.

Elly and I kept our three-person household going thanks to the era's affordable rents, her job at the Women's Center of Brooklyn College (a grassroots feminist organization that provided direct services such as peer counseling), child support payments from her ex, and my haphazard succession of part-time gigs. I set type for a Brooklyn-based community newspaper whose paychecks sometimes bounced and traveled to Manhattan to the CUNY Graduate Center, where I did secretarial work for the snooty feminist scholars at an outfit called the Center for the Study of Women and Sex Roles.

It was a scrappy, strenuous life full of intellectual stimulation and political scut work (oh, those endless meetings!), singularly lacking in the usual demarcations between toil and recreation, artmaking and agitation. Like our foremothers chained to their washboards before the advent of washing machines, we took for granted the sheer amount of physical labor involved in producing, promoting, and distributing *Conditions* in an analog environment. This included everything from detailed snail mail correspondence with contributors—and rejects (I can't recall when, if ever, we sent rejection slips, but we certainly responded with individual letters to many whose work we ended up declining), to preparing copy for our crack freelance typesetter, to creating display ads (mostly used for exchanges with sister publications), to sticking magazines in 6 × 9 in. envelopes, typing and affixing mailing labels, and hauling the load to Van Brunt Station for the handoff to a grumpy but reliable postal clerk. Fortunately for us, there already existed a significant if fragile national infrastructure of women's bookstores, coffeehouses, newspapers, and journals that helped us spread the word and attract more subscribers. Importantly, too, we were able to take advantage of the nascent infrastructure of women's/feminist/gender studies, hawking our wares at the annual conferences of the Modern Language Association and National Women's Studies Association.

It would be years before we had access to any storage space other than our homes. On the glorious day when the truck containing a shipment from our Michigan printer pulled up at curbside ("Where's the loading dock?" the delivery guy barked), lugging the many boxes of magazines up the stoop plus a further three flights to Irena and Rima's apartment gave everyone a workout. It all paid off in the thrill of reading work entrusted to us by a panoply of feminist writers, from our peers among the younger generation of out-and-proud literary dykes to beloved "heavies" like Audre Lorde, Adrienne Rich, Jane Rule, and Alice Walker.

Going to DC on a bus for a major demonstration was a social event; so was hosting a benefit in donated space, or even convening a crew to stuff envelopes for a mailing, as we angled to attract more institutional subscriptions. Our cultural and street activism expanded the pool of women we could approach for a range of contributions, including book reviews—a priority for us given our belief that developing a culture of constructive feminist criticism was crucial to the future of lesbian literature. Doris (later Blue) Lunden—the subject of a lively, revealing interview by Elly that looked back on her youth as a butch, white, working-class dyke in the segregated South—was someone I'd been jailed with when our lesbian affinity group, Dykes Opposed to Nuclear Technology, joined a protest at the Indian Point nuclear power plant in 1979.

Although we had a lot of contacts, we knew it wasn't enough. Our life experiences and social location obviously shaped—at times surely distorted—our editorial judgment; our casual networks reflected the racial and class-based segregation rampant in the culture at large. We understood from the get-go that we'd need to work hard at earning the trust of prospective contributors from backgrounds unlike our own. In my own case, this lesson was clear from my prior work with feminist activist groups like CARASA (the Committee for Abortion Rights and Against Sterilization Abuse), yet I shrank at the thought of possible rejection: could it really be the case, for example, that a brilliant Black lesbian thinker and activist named Barbara Smith would welcome an invitation to write a substantial essay for a white girl-edited magazine? Lo and behold, she did: "Toward a Black Feminist Criticism" (*Conditions: Two*) lays out general criteria for developing a Black feminist approach to literature, demonstrates the need for this approach by citing blatant examples of racist criticism, and famously offers a reading of Toni Morrison's *Sula* as a lesbian text.

With time, we grew uneasy with the limitations of "outreach." We needed to share our ultimate power of editorial control, which we did in a limited way with *Conditions: Five / The Black Women's Issue*, guest-edited by Lorraine Bethel and Barbara Smith. While the four of us agreed in principle that we needed to do more to make the magazine reflect the breadth and depth of women's perspectives invoked in our editorial statement, this was easier said than done. In my view, Elly was often our leader in this regard;

I still recall with admiration how energetically she plunged into a series of friendly/working relationships that broadened our base of support, paving the way for eventual expansion of the editorial collective. This occurred in 1982 with the addition of Dorothy Allison, Cheryl Clarke, Jewelle Gomez, Carroll Oliver, and Mirtha Quintanales. Irena had resigned the previous year, and I also left the collective at this time.

Arguably more important to the magazine's vigor and range than our evolving editorial policy was our fortunate situation in the midst of a lesbian-feminist polito-cultural renaissance. The ecosystem was the thing; cross-fertilization abounded, with many of our contributors deeply immersed in pathbreaking projects of enduring significance. Key examples include the 1981 publication of *This Bridge Called My Back: Writings by Radical Women of Color*, edited by Cherríe Moraga and Gloria Anzaldúa (*Conditions* ran two reviews) and the near-simultaneous founding of Kitchen Table: Women of Color Press. It was in the vicinity of, and deeply influenced by, the ferment engendered by these efforts that *Conditions*' co-founders continued to evolve our views of our own endeavor.

Notes to our readers in *Conditions: Four* and *Seven* shed light on both our shaky finances and our fear of becoming entangled with funders in ways that could compromise our editorial independence. In *Four* (1979), we justified a modest rise in subscription price: "So far, we have kept CONDITIONS afloat with periodic loans from several of the editors. . . . [H]owever, we do not have the personal resources to continue monetary contributions to CONDITIONS indefinitely. We might add that the work of the four editors, as well as that of the guest editors of CONDITIONS: FIVE . . . is strictly unpaid. Writers whose work we publish receive no payment other than two copies of the issue. We expect to continue on this basis for the foreseeable future." By *Seven* (1981), we had received some grant monies that went toward operating expenses, plus an editorial fellowship of $5,000—"the only substantial payment we have received . . . for our editorial work." Though welcome, these infusions of cash made us nervous: "We are painfully aware of the dangers of reliance on outside support, particularly in the present political climate," we explained, alluding to right-wing assaults on cultural expression at the outset of the Reagan administration. With gay and lesbian artists and anyone on the left increasingly in the crosshairs, we had no intention of staking *Conditions'* future on the favor of institutions controlled by our enemies.

In looking back on *Conditions'* conditions, it strikes me that we thrived both because of and despite this uncompromising attitude. Blessed by our insulation from the literary "market," we were under no pressure to chase a mass audience. Going viral wasn't merely out of the question; the very concept hadn't been invented. In keeping a canny distance from funders and institutional agendas, we made a virtue of necessity in a time before the mainstreaming of queer culture and the academic capture of once-insurgent knowledges. With our DIY ethos, we got further than we should have, precisely because we didn't know any better. Given the ways in which our initial approach risked personal exhaustion and financial meltdown, it's amazing to me that we lasted long enough for the expanded collective to be able to retool and reimagine both editorial policy and practical working methods.

In composing these reflections, I've recovered my old sense of the magnitude of what I was able to be part of through my work on *Conditions*: not just a magazine but a movement of sharp critical thinkers, political ethicists, daring poets, and writer-activists who shared the understanding that Barbara Smith spelled out in her "Notes for Yet Another Paper on Black Feminism, Or Will the Real Enemy Please Stand Up" (*Conditions: Five / The Black Women's Issue*)—"I am in essential agreement with the Marxist analysis that it is our material conditions which most clearly affect what we are able to do in our lives" (125)— and who threw themselves into the labor required to transform those conditions in the interests of justice. The work was stressful, with downsides including burnout, heightened tensions between partners and friends, and angry ideological splits of a sort all too familiar to successive generations of radical activists. While my own painful brush with these dynamics had little direct connection with my work on the magazine, I remember how the bitterness carried over, making me more than ready to relinquish my editor's role. I wished the new collective very well from a distance, but felt disengaged. My thoughts about women in groups had taken on a cynical edge. Writing this essay has let me reconnect with my early, ecstatic sense of possibility, which came closer to fulfillment than I recognized at the time.

Conditions was a fortunate, unlikely phenomenon contingent on many factors—above all, the fact that its founding editors worked in a larger context of freedom-bent women whose energy spurred us on. For a lucky interval, threading our way through a forest of constraints, making use of what privilege we possessed, picking up crumbs from under the tables of power, we managed to pry open a space for exploration. What could it mean for women to put women at the center of our lives? In moments, we knew the freedom of making our own culture, all the more precious in light of our understanding that the circumstances under which we did so had never been ours to choose.

Jan Clausen's publications include two novels (*Sinking, Stealing* and *The Prosperine Papers*); the memoir *Apples and Oranges: My Journey through Sexual Identity* (recently reissued by Seven Stories Press); and six volumes of poetry. The latest is the experimental collection *Veiled Spill: A Sequence* (GenPop Books), of which Juliana Spahr says: "Clausen writes of complicated vulnerability and feminist resistance...with such a deep love, with such a lyric invocation." Her poems, creative prose, and critical writing have appeared widely in periodicals spanning the gamut from *AGNI* to *Tarpaulin Sky* and *Jacobin* to *The Women's Review of Books*. An activist in many movements, she taught several generations of creative writers at Eugene Lang College and in the Goddard College MFA in Writing Program. She is working on a memoir of life in desperate times, *My Great Acceleration.*

THE BIOGRAPHICAL FALLACY:
LOOKING BACK AT *CONDITIONS*

Rima Shore

In the mid-seventies, I began graduate school in Russian literature. In the first-year seminar we read essays by numerous critics, but only one literary work: *Feast in the Time of Plague*, Alexander Pushkin's play in verse. It was written in 1830 during Pushkin's stay at his family's country estate that was extended by a cholera epidemic. The professor assigned a series of papers analyzing *Feast* through a full spectrum of critical lenses, which in those days meant formalist, psychological, moral, sociological, and archetypal. I breezed through formalist and psychological, but got stuck on moral.

Feast begins with a group of merrymakers drinking to the memory of a missing friend who has fallen victim to the plague. There was surely a moral thread running through a work about revelry in bleak times, but I kept grasping at it and missing. The feast continues, even as a hearse passes by, and the play ends with the central figure, master of the revels, "lost in thought." Straining to fill in his thoughts, I flipped through a standard life of Pushkin, but we had been warned against the biographical fallacy—the assumption that a literary work reflects the author's own life experience. (Although losing its grip on academia, the New Criticism still held sway in our department. The key idea was that everything needed to get to the heart of a literary work, or to judge its merit, is contained in the words on the page.) Our professor supplied examples of heedless critics who had strayed beyond the text into the minefield of biography. The author of *Crime and Punishment*, he assured us, had not axed his landlady.

I was twenty-six years old. I'd studied Russian for years, and my language skills had improved during several trips to the Soviet

Union and two years' work for a small Russian-language press in New York City. Like my closest friends, I was immersed in all things Russian. Smudged Cyrillic stamps filled the visa pages of my passport, and a portrait of poet Anna Akhmatova hung on the wall. The bulky blue Russian dictionaries piled on my desk were coming unglued.

I lived in Greenwich Village, and the Morton Street townhouse where I rented a studio from a history professor was filled with Russian speakers. My room on the parlor floor had a Pullman kitchen, a brick fireplace, and tall, shuttered windows that gave onto the back garden. From my desk I could often see my downstairs neighbor, Joseph Brodsky, sitting at a small round wrought iron table, hunched over his typewriter. I thought I could tell, from the rhythm of percussive keystrokes, whether he was working on a poem or taking care of correspondence. This was a dozen years before he won the Nobel Prize.

The afternoon before my "moral" paper was due, I took *Feast* upstairs to my friend Masha's apartment to ask for help, but she could see how frazzled I was and suggested a cup of tea. We had just opened the text when Joseph appeared at her door looking for coffee. It was that kind of building. He looked over my shoulder and asked what I was doing.

"It's no mystery," he said in his slightly aggressive English when I explained the assignment. "This was not long after the Decembrist uprising—five years." In December 1825, a group of young officers had demonstrated on St. Petersburg's Senate Square, demanding political reform. Reprisals were swift and harsh. Five were hanged; others were exiled to Siberia or dispatched to remote military outposts. Many were Pushkin's friends. Had he not been hundreds of miles away, at his family estate, he might have joined the insurrection.

"Feasting in a time of plague—it's clear, he is guilty," Brodsky said, meaning, I imagine, that Pushkin had sat out the uprising; he was enjoying a life of comfort while others suffered. Joseph saw in Pushkin's hearse the "Black Maria" coach used by tsarist secret police to transport prisoners.

"Yes," I said, "I see that, but of course there actually was a plague at the time Pushkin was writing it."

"Nevertheless," he said. Brodsky himself had been tried in Leningrad in 1964 for "social parasitism"—benefiting from society without contributing—and was sentenced to internal exile in Russia's rugged far north. In 1972 he was sent to the West—cut off from his motherland, from its living language, from a society where to be a poet is, in every sense, to put one's life on the line. Poet Osip Mandelstam once said of the Soviet Union, "Poetry is respected only in this country—people are killed for it. There's no place where more people are killed for it."

I thanked Joseph for his help, wrote the paper, and got a B. In the margin the professor wrote a single microscopic comment: "Biographical fallacy!"

The following year, a mutual friend introduced me to Irena Klepfisz. Some months later we became a couple, and then—though it was wrenching to leave Morton Street—I moved to Brooklyn. Irena was funny and tender, and she wrote poems that had the beautiful clarity of Akhmatova and Mandelstam. Born in the Warsaw Ghetto, she grew up among Yiddish speakers and was translating poems from Yiddish. Sometimes we would sit together at a small table with our notebooks and dictionaries. Taking breaks, we would prop pillows at the head of the bed and watch *Hawaii Five-O* or *Star Trek*. With uncanny accuracy, Irena would mimic Captain Kirk's voiceover: "Space—the final frontier." When the news came on, she would parody the daily intro to Barbara Walters's new morning show: "Legionnaires' disease—a topic *Not for Women Only!*"

What I recall about that time is an uneasy contentment. Contentment, because life now had a rhythm that matched some inner song that I'd never known was there. And uneasy, because I had such an iffy sense of who I was. Looking back, it seems to me that I was a decidedly young twenty-something. Coming out in my early twenties had taken immense emotional energy, and other parts of my life went unexamined. Whatever the reason, I felt much less clear-eyed than the people around me, who were mostly older than I was. It was confusing that individuals I looked up to—people whose experiences left them with a sensitive moral compass—could have such divergent convictions. My upstairs friend Masha, whose family had suffered terribly when the Red Army occupied Lithuania toward the end of World War II, admired Ronald Reagan because he had shown the courage to call the Soviet Union an evil empire. The men in the Kremlin (and their inheritors, as Masha Gessen has so brilliantly shown) did in fact perpetrate evil, even as their media consistently highlighted US racist violence at home and in Vietnam. My own inherited ideas about "right" and "left" were punctured over and over again.

I see now that I responded by clinging to a practiced naivete. I believed, despite considerable evidence to the contrary, that love affairs last and that things usually turn out all right in the end. I'd grown up in suburban New Jersey with a big noisy family, and I saw no irony in Leo Tolstoy's assurance that all happy families are alike. Okay, we weren't always happy, but nothing I'd experienced stood up to Joseph's arctic exile, Masha's early years in occupied Vilna, or Irena's wartime childhood.

In the stretch between college and grad school, I had earned my keep with my pencil and typewriter—compiling indexes, editing, translating, and publishing a few pieces in newspapers and journals—but if I ever called myself a writer, I stumbled over the word. Irena was unimpressed by this self-doubt. She gave me a serious springback binder for my twenty-seventh birthday and urged me to take my writing out of the drawer and get to work. Before long we got together with another couple, Elly Bulkin and Jan Clausen, to start a literary magazine. My recollection is that the idea took shape over dinner, or over a few dinners. It was 1976. Sinister Wisdom had recently gotten off the ground, and there were a number of other women's periodicals and presses that we respected, but we knew there were still too few outlets for the growing output of writers and critics who identified as lesbians and/or feminists.

To me, this kind of enterprise felt familiar—and familial. My parents worked together in their small business, making hangers and display racks and selling them to clothing stores. During the McCarthy era, they and their friends were fed up with our town's right-leaning newspaper and launched their own, the *Fair Lawn Record.* The editor, a woman named Edna who wore trousers, sat at a desk in a corner of my parents' shop, and I remember tagging along when she went to cover a fire in a local apartment building. I loved being part of a project. My brothers and I formed many clubs in the attic of our house. We once established a bench-building club. We nailed together scraps of lumber to make benches, sat on them, and handed our allowance to my oldest brother, who said we had to pay dues. It was my idea of heaven.

So starting a magazine felt fine. Once we gave it a name, it immediately seemed real. I think we came up with the name at a single meeting. One of us—I don't remember who—suggested *The American Literary Review* on the grounds that "the boys" don't shy away from grandiosity or even notice that their claims are grandiose. But we quickly landed on a different name. *Conditions* was the title of a poem by Irena that we all admired, and it seemed to reflect our shared conviction that context matters. Writing a tagline to describe the magazine was harder. After some negotiation, we decided to call *Conditions* "a magazine of writing by women, with an emphasis on writing by lesbians." (When the collective was expanded in the eighties, the tagline was kept with the addition of the word "feminist.")

The four of us had little money and very little time. Our minutes record that we decided against liability insurance on the grounds that none of us had assets that could be lost in a lawsuit. The workload was onerous. There was no internet and no easy way to reach our audience. To cover start-up costs, we borrowed loft spaces and threw women-only fundraising parties ("more if you can, less if you can't"), serving cheap wine and snacks. The minutes from our weekly meetings amounted to long, meticulous to-do lists. When we met to plan a fundraiser, we even recorded the brand of chips we would serve. With the money we raised, we rented a post office box and hoped that word of mouth, posted announcements, and a few ads would fill it with submissions and subscriptions. Irena and I would often start our day with a six-block walk to check the mail, opening envelopes over a breakfast special ($1.09) at the coffee shop a few doors from the post office.

In time, the post office box began to fill up. We found a typesetter and a printing company, and in the spring of 1977 we published our first issue. We were buoyed by messages from grateful subscribers, encouraging letters from writers we admired, and occasional cash contributions. We opened a bank account. Minutes from an early meeting recall that bookstore sales of our first issue earned us $500 and that another $200 would be forthcoming.

In time, we received grants from the National Endowment for the Arts and New York State Council on the Arts. To reach out to more writers and subscribers, we schlepped flyers and magazines to conferences and spoke on panels. As the work expanded, wildly overqualified women (Cherríe Moraga and Shelley Messing) agreed to work part-time for the magazine, taking some of the administrative work off our hands. Reading our minutes more than forty years later, I'm glad to see that we figured out how to pay their wages, payroll taxes, and health insurance. We rented a tiny, shabby office space. A note in one set of minutes said that if we wanted any work to get done in the office, we would have to stop up the leaks and fix the toilet.

We all had other responsibilities. For me, that meant full-time grad school and part-time teaching. I had comprehensive exams coming up and a dissertation to write. I worried about how I'd manage it all, but I was full of energy and optimism, inspired by the Russian writers who were risking everything to type and circulate carbon copies of *samizdat* (self-published) books and journals. The lesbian world had its own *samizdat* tradition. A few years after graduation, my high school French teacher had lent me an early mimeographed, hand-stapled copy of *The Ladder* (1956–72). I was moved by a letter we received from its longtime editor Barbara Grier, thanking us for helping her make peace with having closed down that pioneering publication.

Between 1977 and 1981 we published seven book-length issues. There were hard times along the way. My relationship with Irena ended. My oldest brother was diagnosed with cancer. I finished my dissertation, but academic jobs in the New York area were scarce. We kept up our weekly meetings. In 1981, when Irena left the collective, Elly, Jan, and I struggled to manage the workload. I recently reread the minutes from a meeting on January 26 of that year ("Day 450 of the Hostage Crisis," our minutes record—ironically, I guess, since it now occurs to me that the crisis ended with Reagan's inauguration a few days earlier). With characteristic piquancy, Jan included in the minutes a final item under the heading *Burnout*:

> Jan announced symptoms of terminal burnout. Rima admitted she has finally realized she can't do all the things she's doing in her life. We agreed on the need for a meeting where we'd feel obliged to do nothing but complain—this to take place when #7 is at [the printers], as we're agreed the show must go on at least that far. Love, let us be true to one another, etc.

And we were true to one another—or tried to be. Year after year, submissions poured into the *Conditions* post office box. At meetings we pushed through old and new business (costs, ads, subscription policies, production glitches, book storage, correspondence, misplaced manuscripts, how to divvy up tasks) so we could finally discuss the poems, stories, essays, and reviews that had been entrusted to us.

From the start, we quickly reached consensus on most submissions. From time to time a submission raised doubts until one or another of us made a strong case for a submission and the rest of us decided we could live with it. Occasionally, consensus eluded us, and we'd leave a meeting frustrated and on edge. Sometimes the two couples were at odds. I recall at least one major blowup over poems that struck me as weak despite being submitted by an author known for principled political activism.

I wonder, was I as conflicted and uncertain as memory suggests? The other editors had a deep earnestness that I admired and were more articulate about their convictions. Their thinking seemed to add up to a coherent worldview. There were sharp differences among them, to be sure, but they shared a view of literary texts as inseparable from the experiences and identities of those who created them. Crucial to identity was the sensibility and outlook that came from being part of a group, or several overlapping groups. There was a growing awareness of the power dynamics among those groups. As the eighties approached, we began to speak of identity politics—and looking back, I can see the outlines of ideas that would develop into principles like *positionality* and *intersectionality*. Elly and Irena were among the contributors writing incisively about Jewish identity. Audre Lorde, an early contributor, defined herself not only as a poet, but also as a "black lesbian warrior mother." She wrote, "If I didn't define myself for myself, I would be crunched into other people's fantasies for me and eaten alive." In the poem "New Year's Day," Lorde had written, "I am deliberate / and afraid / of nothing." She believed in an urgent activist poetry that "lays the foundations for a future of change, a bridge across our fears of what has never been before."

I felt stranded on that bridge. To begin with, I was indecisive, and I feared missteps. I wasn't sure how a writer's life and work fit together exactly, or who could say how they should. The New Criticism made no sense to me; surely there was more to a poem or prose piece than its verbal texture, its imagery, or even its standalone ideas. At the same time, I resisted the vibrating Venn diagrams that I felt circling around me as identity politics took hold. I was certainly part of a generation, and I had glimmers of what it meant to have grown up in a white suburb. I felt keenly a sense of shared destiny with other women, lesbians, Jews (and later, mothers and grandmothers). My father and all of my grandparents had immigrated to the US from shtetls in Poland or Russia, and their journeys indelibly marked my own path. Yes, there were groups I belonged to and identified with, but it troubled me that our community placed so little weight on the one group in which I felt most strongly rooted: family.

Why, in retrospect, is no mystery. We launched *Conditions* not long after the Stonewall uprising—seven years. The modern march toward LGBTQ rights had just begun, and once rumors of a gay plague started to circulate, we had reason to fear that there would be roadblocks. As the scope of the AIDS epidemic became evident, the hostility around us was palpable; whatever strides we had made toward acceptance (and self-acceptance) were clearly at risk. I was fortunate—my family stood by me, but many in our community were hurt by their families, some shunned, some marginalized, others embraced but pitied or patronized. We were hard at work constructing families of choice—constellations of lovers, former lovers, friends, and children. All of that was very real to me, but somehow it didn't add up to a worldview. It just made me homesick.

From the start, we had wanted our magazine to fully credit context—the conditions in which we lived, loved, and worked. I shared that goal, but I was wary of an activist literature. My thinking about this sharpened when we received, in the *Conditions* PO box, an essay on feminist writing arguing that writers who benefit from the movement must be "accountable to the movement," taking political stances that move it forward. I kept a carbon copy of my three-page response questioning that premise. In it, I talked about the ideological tests faced by Russian writers. I offered the closer-to-home example of a woman whose superb work was highly personal, not political in the conventional sense, and who was having trouble finding outlets in our feminist print world. Despite the catchphrase that the personal is political, our literary outlets favored work that floated far enough above the minutiae of daily life to reveal and identify the underlying power dynamics.

I suffered over that letter; I can tell from its pile of overworked paragraphs. I was conscious of the ways I had benefited from the feminist and gay liberation movements, and the notion of accountability resonated with me. But I still had Anna Akhmatova's portrait hanging over my desk, and I asked myself whether feminist presses would have rejected her lyric poems as apolitical and lightweight. I could picture her self-addressed stamped envelope. At magazine meetings, as we considered submissions, I found myself puzzling once again over the moral approach and what it required of us. I doubted that it called upon us to rise above messy experience or to step back from emotional specificity. I was, of course, joining in the day's consciousness-raising conversations about the forces that shape women's lives, but as a reader and editor, I was drawn to the close-up view, to work that explored and conveyed the textures of women's lives. Meanwhile, in grad school, women students were urged to turn our binoculars around for a distanced, detached take on whatever we studied. We could see that the feminist scholars most likely to get jobs and promotions were setting their sights on theoretical discourse, taking up subject matter that was "Not for Women Only." In the end, I didn't feel completely at home in the feminist literary world or in academia.

Looking back, I feel compassion, even admiration, for the waffling editor I was forty years ago. Russia's literary history has brought home to me the calamities that follow from the certainty of being right. Weren't literary arbiters with boundless confidence in their political instincts responsible for hounding Akhmatova, killing Mandelstam, exiling Brodsky?

Over the years, I've thought about the magazine and my Soviet adventures as separate. They inhabit different drawers of a very old file cabinet. The stories I've told my family—the Russia stories and the *Conditions* stories—must seem like they come from different eras, but it was all happening at the same time. Often I felt paralyzed. I had Anna Akhmatova looking over one shoulder and Audre Lorde looking over the other.

It's clear from the stack of *Conditions* on my shelf that I was trying to reconcile these two lives. I see my essay about the forgotten Russian lesbian poet Sophia Parnok, a story set in a Soviet maternity clinic, and a one-act play about my uncle, a Moscow airplane designer. The essay "Sisterhood and My Brothers," published in *Conditions*: *Eight*, was out of step with 1970s lesbian orthodoxy. I reread all of these pieces as a shameless practitioner of the biographical fallacy.

As Jan had anticipated, the show did go on. We addressed, belatedly I think, the impossibility of continuing the magazine as a collective of white women. Turning over *Conditions: Five* to guest editors Lorraine Bethel and Barbara Smith for a Black Women's Issue was a meaningful gesture, but lending our magazine to others proved more complicated than we had imagined when a poem that was accepted for publication contrasted Black and Jewish experience in a very problematic way. Who was accountable? And to whom? That history is, as the Russians say, a song from a different opera, and I leave it to others to tell it. Suffice it to say that a way forward was found. *Conditions: Five* reached more readers than any of our previous issues and was considered a landmark in feminist publishing, but in the end, our Band-Aid solution to the problem of an all-white collective was no solution at all.

In January 1981, five writers we admired—Dorothy Allison, Cheryl Clarke, Jewelle Gomez, Carroll Oliver, and Mirtha Quintanales—joined the *Conditions* collective, and the magazine was revitalized. I didn't know what to expect once we were a bigger, more diverse group, but immediately meetings became less predictable, more interesting, and more relaxed. We shifted to publishing one issue a year, and we were less harried. Minutes from the early 1980s continued to divvy up scores of tasks, but also mentioned serving cornbread in abundance, listening to Otis Redding and Aretha Franklin, and gathering around a glowing fireplace.

New business at our March 12, 1983, meeting included my plan to leave the magazine after our ninth issue. I don't remember exactly what prompted the decision, but what jumps out at me now is the date—ten days after my brother's death at age thirty-eight. I was exhausted and heartbroken, but I also felt confident that our work would be carried on.

Conditions was more successful than we could have predicted at those early dinners in Brooklyn; it kept going until 1990, resulting in seventeen issues. We drew a remarkable array of contributors and worked hard to produce a vehicle that would honor their work and their courage. We handed *Conditions* off to an amazing group of women who expanded and deepened the original vision. What I'm left with, looking back, is the knowledge that the work we published heartened and inspired many readers. For those who have succeeded us in the sphere of lesbian-feminist publishing, that remains true.

Author's note:

The prose quotes from Audre Lorde are taken from her 1982 speech at Harvard University entitled "Learning from the '60s" (http://www.blackpast.org/1982-audre-lorde-learning-60s), and from "Poetry Is Not a Luxury," published in *Chrysalis* no. 3, 1977, and republished in *Sister Outsider: Essays and Speeches by Audre Lorde* (Berkeley: Crossing Press, 1984, p. 38).

The "way forward," arrived at before *Conditions: Five* was published, involved adding this footnote to Judy Simmons's poem "Minority": "The editors of *Conditions: Five* went through a difficult process in deciding to publish 'Minority' because of the way in which it raises issues about political and personal relationships between Black and Jewish people, particularly Black and Jewish women. Feminists are currently confronting the problems of both racism and antisemitism in the women's movement. As a result of the discussion initiated by this poem, we and the ongoing editors of *Conditions* feel that it is important to encourage dialogue between Black and Jewish women. The ongoing editors plan to publish an article based upon one such discussion in a forthcoming issue of *Conditions*."

Rima Shore is the author of *Lady with a Brooch—Violinist Eva Mudocci: A Biography and a Detective Story* (2019).

SINISTER WISDOM'S *CONDITIONS* MAGAZINE TRIBUTE

Barbara Smith

Long before the internet, print was the medium that allowed women to communicate across geographic boundaries and to access lifesaving information, inspiration, and tools for both personal and political transformation. Nowadays it seems to be taken for granted that queer and trans women of color are invited to grace the covers and provide editorial content for slick commercial magazines. This level of access has a history, however, that is rooted in the vision, passionate commitment, and sacrifice of those who created the presses, bookstores, publications, and movements that paved the way and blew open the doors.

I already knew about *Conditions* and had read the first issue when I was contacted about writing for the magazine. I had recently met Adrienne Rich through her sister, Cynthia Rich, who lived in the Boston area. Adrienne had contributed to *Conditions: One* and suggested to the editors that I might be a possible contributor.

I received a letter from Elly Bulkin dated April 26, 1977, inviting me to contribute an article to *Conditions: Two*. She wrote:

We would like to include in the next issue of *Conditions* a survey article on contemporary writing by Black women and wonder if you'd be interested in writing it. . . .

We realize, of course, that many articles could—and should—be written on this topic and that some focus would be needed for the *Conditions* article. Although we view the exact topic and approach as your own, we did talk about the possibility of an overview of fiction by Black women writers, a look at Black lesbians in fiction, an overview of Black women's/lesbian poetry, and a discussion of the role of Black women in small presses. All of these topics would require further narrowing down, since we have space for an article of 15–20 pages double-spaced with a bibliography at the end. I want to stress that we view these as *possible* topics. We would welcome additional suggestions.

During the mid-1970s I was teaching African American literature and women's studies, including courses on Black women writers, at Emerson College and the University of Massachusetts, Boston. In 1975 I co-founded the Combahee River Collective. I was a member of the Modern Language Association Commission on the Status of Women in the Profession and had conceptualized a book about Black women's studies that began as an MLA-supported project. I mention these activities because they are some of the experiences that influenced the approach I decided to take in "Toward a Black Feminist Criticism" in response to *Conditions*' open-ended suggestions.

I felt that instead of doing a survey of writing by Black women, there was first a pressing need to define the field of Black women's literature. Although it may be difficult to imagine now, Black women writers with few exceptions were extremely marginalized, if not completely ignored. There was no understanding that Black women's literature could be a distinct, legitimate focus of research, criticism, and teaching. There was nothing that I was aware of that laid out the parameters of the field, described the challenges faced by the handful of those of us who were committed to establishing the field, or outlined characteristics and themes of Black women's writing. There was definitely no acknowledgement of Black lesbians in literature or of Black lesbian writers.

I had a very positive experience working with the *Conditions* editors. They did not shy away from looking at the consequences of the intertwined oppressions of race, class, gender, and sexuality, and unlike many feminist and lesbian publications, they wanted the magazine to reflect those challenging political realities.

"Toward a Black Feminist Criticism" received a lot of attention both in the academy and in the larger women's movement. It is the most frequently reprinted essay among all of my work, and it has been translated into several languages. I was delighted when Jan Clausen, one of the *Conditions* editors who had started her own press, decided to publish it as a Long Haul Press pamphlet so that it could reach an even wider audience.

In December 1977 the *Conditions* editors invited Akasha (Gloria) Hull and me to co-edit a Black women's issue, *Conditions: Five.* Although Akasha initially accepted, she realized that she needed to withdraw because of her other responsibilities. I wanted to work with a co-editor, which the *Conditions* editors supported, so I invited Lorraine Bethel, to whom I had been introduced by my sister Beverly Smith. They had met at Yale when Lorraine was in college and Beverly was in graduate school.

An excerpt from the editors' invitation letter to Akasha and me reflects their antiracist perspective. They wrote:

> As guest editors you would have complete editorial control over the issue. We are clear that this is essential even though it feels a bit difficult to contemplate relinquishing our hold on a project with which each of us is so closely identified. We see your editorship of an issue of Black women's writing as a response to the inevitable problems associated with white editors passing judgment on Black writers. We have a great deal of respect for your work, and would be excited to see an issue put together by you.

Editing *Conditions: Five* was both exciting and a tremendous undertaking. It was published in the late fall of 1979. The *Conditions* editors printed a lot more copies than usual, anticipating high demand. They were right. The first printing sold out very quickly and a second printing followed. Recently on Twitter, someone posted the table of contents of *Conditions: Five* and described it as a who's who of Black women writers. Although there were some luminaries among the contributors, most of them were still early in their careers, and for some *Conditions: Five* was their first publication.

Conditions: Five was the first major collection of explicitly Black feminist and Black lesbian writing published in the United States. My recollection is that it eventually sold 10,000 copies, which is astounding for such a small, volunteer-run operation. Because I wanted the writing to continue to be available, I decided to turn it into a book. A lot of the work in *Conditions: Five* is included in *Home Girls: A Black Feminist Anthology*, originally published by Kitchen Table: Women of Color Press.

I contributed a couple of other articles and reviews to *Conditions*. One of them, co-authored with my sister Beverly, was "Letters from Black Feminists" in *Conditions: Four*.

Overall, *Conditions* magazine had significant impact upon feminist literature and the feminist movement. Its consistently high literary quality and its willingness to engage with the politics of race and class made it stand out. My association with *Conditions* also led to a lifelong friendship with Elly Bulkin, one of the founding editors. Having the opportunity to work with the magazine was incredibly important to my career as a young writer.

Barbara Smith is an author, activist, and independent scholar who has played a groundbreaking role in opening up a national cultural and political dialogue about the intersections of race, class, sexuality, and gender. She was among the first to define an African American women's literary tradition and to build Black women's studies and Black feminism in the United States. She has been politically active in many movements for social justice since the 1960s. Her career is documented in *Ain't Gonna Let Nobody Turn Me Around: Forty Years of Movement Building with Barbara Smith* (SUNY Press).

Smith was a cofounder of the Combahee River Collective in 1975 and of Kitchen Table: Women of Color Press in 1981, the first US publisher for women of color to reach a wide national audience. She served two terms as a member of the city council in Albany, New York from 2006 to 2013. In 2005, she was nominated for the Nobel Peace Prize.

CONDITIONS: UN-CONDITIONING OURSELVES
Melinda Goodman

By the late 1970s, the "women's movement" was so overrun by straight white bourgeois women that it alienated those of us who were deeply committed to LGBTI, antiracist, anti-imperialist struggle. African American lesbian-feminists like Audre Lorde and the Combahee River Collective openly addressed the racist elements in works such as those by feminist writers Susan Brownmiller and Mary Daly. Unfortunately, Lorde's brilliant "Open Letter to Mary Daly" did not seem to be able to break through the aggressive and passive-aggressive walls of what has come to be known as "white fragility."

Around that time, my college professor, Dr. Gloria I. Joseph, and her student assistant, Carroll Oliver, invited Audre Lorde to visit two of our classes: "Racism, Sexism, and Monopoly Capitalism" and "Black Women/White Women." Audre Lorde, who introduced herself as a "Black Lesbian Mother Warrior Poet," had a powerful presence, and we gravitated to her just as she gravitated to us. Many years later, Dr. Joseph edited a book about Audre Lorde called "The Wind Is Spirit," a title that recognized all the ways in which Audre Lorde was (and continues to be) "the perfect storm" for bursting through a very stagnant, confusing, and hurtful time. The '70s, in fact, had become what Gil Scott-Heron called "Winter in America"—a time when "all of the healers have been killed or sent away." But then Audre Lorde stepped up with her African American woman's revolutionary intelligence, creativity, determination, courage, compassion, and leadership skills—she was the embodiment of what later became known as "intersectionality"—insisting she needed to be all of who she was regardless of whether others were able to deal with her Blackness, her Queerness, her Woman-ness, her Poet-ness, her Badass-ness, or whatever she was bringing to the table. She made a point of defining herself for herself instead of trying to dilute, diminish, and mold herself into something that was more comfortable for those who thought they knew what she was supposed to be. Audre Lorde said, "The master's tools will never dismantle the master's house" . . . which is why she proclaimed, "Poetry is not a luxury." Real change will only come about when we let go of the dominant patriarchal Eurocentric ways of being, behaving, responding, and perceiving. Therefore, one of her most immediate demands was that poets and poetry be front and center in all activist projects and activities.

> It is within this light that we form those ideas by which we pursue our magic and make it realized. This is poetry as illumination, for it is through poetry that we give name to those ideas which are, until the poem, nameless and formless-about to be birthed, but already felt. That distillation of experience from which true poetry springs births thought as dream births concept, as feeling births idea, as knowledge births (precedes) understanding.
> —Audre Lorde 1985, "Poetry is Not a Luxury" (1985)

My first introduction to *Conditions* was in January of 1979 with *Conditions: Five / The Black Women's Issue. Conditions: Five* was so groundbreaking that years later, in 1988, when I was offered an opportunity to join the *Conditions* editorial collective, I jumped at the chance.

The reality of the work was not as glamorous as I'd imagined, but I was glad to be a lesbian poet who was taking an active role in expanding my own consciousness as part of the growing LGBTI movement. The *Conditions* collective members were a diverse and dedicated group. We met regularly and divided up manuscript submissions and necessary tasks. I had a hard time rejecting submissions of hopeful writers because I knew what it felt like to have my writing turned down. It was challenging, and we all were doing it for free while we continued to work at our regular jobs.

At *Conditions*, I learned what goes into editing and producing a manuscript for publication, and then I learned what goes into getting the books into the mail to be delivered to all our subscribers. It takes maturity and alertness to persist despite the pulls of everyday life and the potential damage of personal ego disruptions/eruptions that can destroy even our best creative efforts.

Mostly, I learned what it is to be "a collective." We were kind to each other—respectful and conscientious. We showed up on time and were grateful to each other when members contributed extra work, time, and resources. It was one of the best cultural/political collaborations I ever joined, and I am especially grateful for the sensitive care that was shown to me by Audre Lorde and the *Conditions* collective during the year my father died of pancreatic cancer. As Lorde said, "Without community there is no liberation."

My biggest regret is that we couldn't do more to wrap our arms around all the other people who submitted their work to us, who published with us, who subscribed to *Conditions*, who read our journal, and who came to our fundraisers and collaborative events, such as our readings at The Center on Thirteenth Street with Men of All Colors Together (MACT). The late '80s were not easy times for a community that was hanging on by its fingernails through endless personal and collective tragedies due to such forces as the AIDS crisis, mass incarceration of people of color, cancer, depression, domestic violence, sexual abuse, addiction, racist/sexist/homophobic/ableist/ageist/looksist brainwashing and violence, police terror, and poverty. We did what we could as a small volunteer group of writers who were standing on the courageous shoulders of many known and unknown activist forebears.

One important choice we made was deciding that the journal should have a more international representation. For me, this decision was further influenced by Audre's involvement with a group of Afro-German women whom she'd met in Berlin while undergoing alternative cancer treatments. It was also around this time that Lorde and Dr. Joseph founded a group, with South African activist and writer Ellen Kuzwayo, called Sisters in Support of Sisters in South Africa (SISSSA).

Meanwhile, we at *Conditions* were doing all of our work through snail mail and landline telephones. A fax machine and an answering machine were still considered high tech. We did layouts for flyers by hand and had to get thousands printed up. None of us left a meeting without a bag full of leaflets to post and distribute. Back then, progressive literary journals didn't charge writers to submit their work, and if a prospective contributor didn't provide a SASE ("self-addressed stamped envelope") we would use our own postage to get back in touch.

I'm glad that I worked with the collective at a time of bricks and mortar—when we held real paper manuscripts in our hands and worried about spilling coffee all over them. I'm glad we had to meet face-to-face and hear each other's voices and go to each other's apartments. I miss these women poets, and our groans and laughter at all we had to do with no money and not enough time. When I look back, I feel like I did very little compared with the heavy hitters like Cheryl Clarke, who had been in the collective much longer and knew about getting grants and, in general, getting things done to bring out another volume of *Conditions*.

Currently, I am recovering from COVID-19 and dealing with autoimmune health issues while helping to care for my ninety-two-year-old mother. I am also in my thirty-third year teaching creative writing as an adjunct (hired semester-by-semester on a low-paying "contingency" basis with no job security and only minimal benefits). As anyone reading this can attest, life can be extremely lonely and scary at times. When I got Julie's email asking me to write about my time working with *Conditions*, it knocked me out of my morning feeling of isolation, and I immediately started tapping out this response on the glass window of my phone.

In closing, I want to thank Cheryl Clarke and the other women I worked with at that time for making it a meaningful and satisfying experience: Mariana Romo-Carmona, Dorothy Randall Gray, Paula Martinac, and Pam A. Parker. Working with the *Conditions* editorial collective was my way of making what the late congressman and freedom fighter John Lewis called "good trouble"—meaning, it focused my energy in a very positive, nurturing, revolutionary way at a time when I was losing my flow to overwhelming pain and confusion.

Finally, I want to dedicate the words I've written here today to Terri Jewelle and Donna Allegra—two fierce, brilliant Black lesbian poets who have joined the "An-sisters" and whose bravery, creativity, love, and life force will be expanding our collective consciousness for many years to come.

Melinda Susan Goodman was in the *Conditions* editorial collective from *Conditions: Fifteen* (1988) through *Conditions: Seventeen* (1990). She is a lesbian activist, poet, writer, painter, theater director, and filmmaker who teaches creative writing at Hunter College of the City University of New York. She has received fellowships and awards from the Astraea Foundation, Columbia University, the New York Foundation on the Arts, and the Key West Literary Seminar. Her work has appeared in numerous LGBTI publications. Most recently she has completed a poetry manuscript entitled "Where the Dust Lies."

CONDITIONS CHANGE

Randye Lordon

When I joined the *Conditions* (*Thirteen*) collective in the 1980s, the world was a vastly different place.

Knowing that I was gay from the age of seven had not made me a brave woman like the women who had created and shaped *Conditions* a uniquely wonderful force. In fact, when Cheryl approached me, I was concerned I could never live up to the women who had stood up to be heard while I just paused on the sidelines and cheered.

Back then, while I was out to my family and friends, I was missing an element I knew these other women shared, *must* have shared—confidence in who they were, what they were. They were loud. They were proud. I was just loud (Jewish family: we're all loud).

They were unconditionally lesbians who offered no apology for who they were, and here they had asked me—a woman toying with a book idea with the working title *Homophobic Homosexuals*, because it best described not only me but also a huge culture at that time. Maybe still. Yes, still. Because the condition of humankind today is much as it has been since the beginning of time. Oh, sure, the evolution of how we live, communicate, and travel is at the other end of the spectrum, but essentially people have not changed. At the very center of our core is the kernel of insecurity that manifests differently for each of us. But manifest it does. One can turn it inward or out. Creative or destructive. Use a gun or a pen.

Those courageous, articulate women who started *Conditions*, and then those who were on the collective with me, the women who submitted poetry and prose who stood up and out—they all had their kernels, but they insisted on being heard.

I heard them. I joined their voices and actions with my own. But I never felt fully a part of the sisterhood: my little kernel of insecurity was determined to trip me up. And in some ways, it did.

I have never chosen well in love. I let others make decisions that were mine to make. And I have slipped into shadows when the spotlight was right there waiting for me. But, like the women I learned from, I stood strong.

When my first book, featuring lesbian private investigator Sydney Sloane, was making the rounds of publishers, I was asked to make a decision that changed the path of my life.

Back then you could send a manuscript over the transom to publishers, and I did. In the meantime, I managed to get one of the most formidable agents in the mystery genre to represent me.

Then a day writers dream about—lunch at the Four Seasons with my agent and the publisher of Simon & Schuster. The publisher was lovely, certainly someone to have a crush on, and when she suggested I make Sydney initially straight, a woman who finds her way to loving women as the series progresses, I was amenable to the change.

But over the course of lunch, I listened to my agent argue the merits of Sydney being gay, and they were the very reasons I had written the book in the first place. I had to agree with him. The whole objective was to create a series with a gay woman that bridged the gap between gay and straight readers. I turned down an offer from a publishing company I would have otherwise given my left arm to work with.

It was at that precise moment I knew I had quietly, and perhaps to my own professional detriment, stood tall and stood out, not just for a cause but for myself. I believe I could do that in part because of my short time with the *Conditions* collective. I may have been a homophobic homosexual, but time spent with such talented women like Jewelle Gomez—one among many—gave me, I think, a bar to rise to.

What I didn't know as I walked away from the Four Seasons in a jumble of mixed feelings was that my book *Brotherly Love* had slipped over one of the publishing transoms and found a home with St. Martin's Press.

Back then gay lit was relegated to a piece of a shelf in most bookstores, so I was determined to introduce myself and ask them to please display *Brotherly Love* in the mystery section, not (or not just) in lesbian literature. My objective was to cross the barrier. I must have logged a mile of pacing in front of some stores before I could broker the courage to go in and ask for something from someone who didn't know me. Sometimes it worked out (the Upper West Side Barnes & Noble gave me a window) and sometimes it didn't, especially with independents who were always welcoming but didn't have the shelf space to scatter me hither and yon.

Conditions have changed since *Conditions* was published. Never did I expect that in my lifetime same-sex marriages would be legal, and gender-bending just might be the one thing that brings social unity in another hundred years.

I won't be here to see it, but it is the one thing, the only thing, that makes me hopeful for the future.

Many years from now, when the topography of the planet is much changed, when Colorado lines the Pacific coast and Manhattan is the new Atlantis, those left will have evolved into a baseline of tolerant societies, and that will have been born from the tenacity of feminists and the LGBTQ community.

When I was asked to participate in this tribute, I said yes, and then the kernel of insecurity started tapping to be heard. I have written several iterations of this essay, all of which were either too self-conscious, too serious, or too political. All I wanted to do was write about how *Conditions* affected me.

Conditions was a starting line for my life in many ways. I was surrounded by a group of women who lived within a culture that was mine but one in which I'd not yet integrated. *Conditions* helped me step into my future as an unashamed gay woman.

Standing at this end of the path and looking back thirty years, I find comfort in knowing that change is constant, and conditions will constantly change. But I will always be grateful for the *Conditions* that challenged me on all levels. In the end we created something that makes us proud.

Randye Lordon is the author of the award-winning Sydney Sloane mystery series that explores family relationships vis-à-vis murder. Originally from Chicago, Randye moved to Manhattan where she graduated from the American Academy of Dramatic Arts. It was a logical jump from acting to writing. Aside from her novels, Lordon's short stories have been published in mystery magazines, anthologies, and newspapers, and recorded for a Canadian radio station. She resides now in East Hampton where she is an innkeeper and considers murder daily.

INTERNATIONAL PERSPECTIVE: THE TRANSFORMATIVE CONDITION OF THE *CONDITIONS* FEMINIST JOURNAL

Mariana Romo-Carmona

W hy books? Why have so many movements been propelled in the modern age by the pages of a book produced independently, in the margins, outside the mainstream? From innovation in the arts to the struggle for social change, our access to digital media today can be traced as reverberations of those print publications: small, interstitial[1] events, that represented sometimes subtle but significant shifts.

Conditions, the journal, is a remarkable publication that began as a conversation in a political territory defined by activists in the New York area through the twentieth-century civil rights movement and second-wave feminism; and *Conditions*, the collective, seen as a continuum of effort by writers, is a part of history that we can read in the pages of the journal as it underwent important transformations. To my mind, it is the multiplicity of experience and thought, expressed in their premier issue as a note to the reader, that reflects the significance of a journal that functioned from the very start from a decentered position. The note in the 1977 issue, *Conditions: One*, by Elly Bulkin, Jan Clausen, Irena Klepfisz, and Rima Shore, the founding editors, acknowledges this crucial difference: "We have found that the four of us do not always agree or identify with viewpoints expressed by the women we publish, or with each other." These writers asserted

---

1 While this is not a theoretical article, I would like to acknowledge that the concept of a sociopolitical interstice has been utilized in other contexts by others, including Gloria Anzaldúa, María Lugones, Gilles Deleuze, Homi Bhabha, and Hamid Naficy. I develop the concept of an interstitial enunciation as a sociopolitical and cultural influence in my work on the poetry of Carlos de Rokha during the Chilean Vanguard period in the 1930s.

that they "do not proceed from a single conception" and, with this acknowledgment, I believe they were preparing an implicit territory for change.[2]

The most notable shift was *Conditions: Five / The Black Women's Issue*, published in 1979 and co-edited by guest editors Lorraine Bethel and Barbara Smith.[3] Just as significant were the changes that led to a new collective with *Conditions: Nine* (1982), and later the *International Issues: I and II* (*Conditions: Thirteen* and *Fourteen*), which contained several entries translated into English. At this juncture, the journal was following the mandate of the editors who had produced the previous issue—to focus on the work of women outside the US

Conditions: Thirteen is an impressive collection that features work by women from thirteen countries, including Puerto Rico and the United States. As it was published at the end of the United Nations Decade for Women, the focus is notably on systemic violence against women, from sterilization abuse to sexual trafficking and rape. AIDS, right-wing censorship, and apartheid are also universal concerns, and the entries of fiction and poetry speak with the power and eloquence of writers that seem united against common oppressions. Rereading these pieces now would show how important the reader's perspective is in being able to hear the changing rhythms of familiar US writers—Sapphire and Marilyn Hacker, for instance—against the newer sounds of the poet gracepoore from Malaysia, or Jessica Hagedorn, whose novel *Dogeaters* about Filipino experience would be published four years later, in 1990. While readers in the US had come to expect the literary excellence and the innovative variety of *Conditions*, in other parts of the world the interview with two South Asian lesbians using pseudonyms, by Susan Heske, would have been an astonishing achievement and an occasion for celebration by

---

2 Elly Bulkin et al., eds., *Conditions: One*, 1977, 3.

3 Bethel, Lorraine, and Barbara Smith. Eds. *Conditions: five*. New York, 1982.

lesbian activists. The title, "There Are, Always Have Been, Always Will Be Lesbians in India," might appear to say it all, but that would not do it justice. Utsa and Kayal cover topics such as classical poetry from the sixth century BCE with mention of love between women, the effect of British colonial rule, the contemporary feminist movement in India, and their views on mainstream US lesbian communities, to name just four.

The collection deserves a much more detailed critical reading, there's no question, and all hyperbole aside, I would also argue that it strengthens the position of *Conditions* as one of the best journals of the time. With high-quality poetry and fiction, as well as a groundbreaking interview, *Conditions: Thirteen* is an extremely valuable resource in our archives today. In addition, it contains fifteen book reviews whose subjects include *I. . . Rigoberta Menchú: An Indian Woman*, by Menchú and Elizabeth Burgos-Debray, and the anthology *Gaptooth Girlfriends: The Third Act*, with an introduction by Alexis De Veaux.

After the first international issue, the collective met in September of 1986 to talk about seeking new members, a move that, common to the building and growing of collectives, means that there were crucial changes taking place. It is not a simple or painless process to have members leave or join a collective, to recognize that it is time to move on to new work, or to make room for new people with different ideas. Sometime later that year, or possibly early in 1987, I met with Cheryl Clarke, an editor since *Conditions: Nine*, to discuss the translation of poems by the Cuban poet Minerva Salado from Spanish into English for *Conditions: Fourteen*.

As a former editor with Kitchen Table Press, I had co-edited *Cuentos: Stories by Latinas*[4] with Alma Gómez and Cherríe Moraga (Gómez et al.), and I knew Cheryl Clarke as the author of *Narratives:*

---

4 Alma Gómez, Cherríe Moraga, and Mariana Romo-Carmona, eds., *Cuentos: Stories by Latinas* (Kitchen Table: Women of Color Press, 1983).

poems in the tradition of black women,[5] which had been distributed by Kitchen Table. Even as a member of many such groups, I didn't realize then, meeting over the text of Salado's poems in a narrow Manhattan coffee shop, how the inner workings of the collective endeavor called *Conditions: A Feminist Journal* were being transformed. These are shifts that become apparent much later, when we understand that books and everything and everyone that goes around them, compose an organism. *Conditions: Fourteen* was published in 1987, continuing the vision of *Thirteen*, but also committing to a global scope as an intrinsic part of the journal.

In translating Minerva Salado's poems, I understood my contribution to be part of the trajectory for Latin American and Caribbean writers and Latina/o writers in the US, one that presented work in a bilingual format, often part of a hybrid publication as *Cuentos* had been. It broke with the monolingual standards and assumptions of the US publishing industry because it claimed a territory in which Spanish could be read as a language of original creation, not merely translation. This was the strength of the shift that was taking place in Latinx literature in the US; it was a shift that decentered the first-world perspective and demanded from the reader an assumption of literary hybridity and multilingual publications as well as multicultural, or global, feminisms. When *Conditions: Fourteen* came out, I was rather amazed to see that it contained several translations of poems by Latina and Latin American poets, as well as essays about the conditions of women internationally. Since I had been a contributing translator but had not worked on the issue, it was a gratifying experience to see a journal that contained both English and Spanish. Soon afterwards, I was invited to join the editorial board of the collective, to become part of the transforming *Conditions* editorial board that met at the legendary

---

5 Cheryl Clarke, *Narratives: Poems in the Tradition of Black Women* (Sister Books, 1982).

Peacock Café in the Village, as did many poets and writers over the years, both the famous and the unknown.

As a new editor, then, I began working on *Conditions: Fifteen*, the issue that would appear in 1988. This meant continuing the tasks that had become a sort of tradition for small presses and independent journals: taking turns picking up the mail at the Brooklyn post office, sorting the submissions and inquiries from writers at the small, cluttered office, and responding by mail once again to writers who sent us their work and other small presses who sent their books for review. There is a dialogical process that happens in that exchange of texts between writers, editors, and publishers, one that can extend over months—even years—and must, if the editors are willing, begin to transform the nature and the content of intellectual dialogue. As a Latin American writer, born and raised in Chile, I was an immigrant in the US, and in becoming a writer I had become a Latina, an activist, once I recognized my political identity. Today, knowing that young people in Chile have been the leading force behind the referendum to rewrite the national constitution by a plebiscite vote of nearly 80 percent, I know that participating in marches and demonstrations most definitely changes who we are—but working on and producing books begins to change and expand the canvas of history, where we all (hopefully) begin to see ourselves. To expand the canvas so it can hold the memories of the time when *Conditions* emerged, we have to imagine a horizon. The horizon is necessary in order to position ourselves in relation to who we were and what was happening at the time.

Too often, considerations of people's lives with regard to their struggle, their actions of resistance, and the enunciations of their voices are simply not part of the picture. As women and lesbians in April of 1977, the editors of *Conditions: One* were sketching out their existence upon that canvas. As Black women in 1979, the editors of *Conditions: Five* were bringing in images and perspectives that had not included them before, even on the feminist horizon that many of us glimpsed from the vantage point of our communities. Today, in the wake of a global protest of the murder of Black and Indigenous people of color by police, we know how people have struggled to fill that canvas with images and experiences until it can contain our humanity. Over the years, poring over the table of contents, it is possible to trace from the first issue the poems by Black women, the first poems by women identifying as Jews, as lesbians, as poets born in Greece or Italy, or Cuba, the first reviews of books by Black writers, the first poems that contained names of places in parts of the world other than the United States, the first words in languages other than English— including the first poem printed in Spanish in the first issue, even if all the accents were entered by hand upon the typeset letters. Just as an example, for Latinas, the use of diacritical marks in Spanish on a typeset page would have meant the acknowledgment of difference, the use of a subaltern language in the United States for which there are no accents or tildes on keyboards, and reminds speakers of these languages that they, along with their writing, are not seen, or read in established publications. These accents mean recognition of experience and humanity.

But, just for a moment, let us think once more about what it would have been like when the canvas, any canvas, any book, any mural, any photograph, any chorus of voices upon a stage seemed to be empty of so many people? How, where, and with what tools would we begin to fill it with the conditions of our lives?

I was one of those people who had lived far away in a rural area, beyond the margins, not knowing how my experience as an immigrant connected to the changing communities around me. There was, however, a horizon of activism for social change, and I had been gravitating toward it. From the wilds of eastern Connecticut, where the source of news was Pacifica Radio that arrived at the university radio station by mail, recorded on thick, vinyl records, to the anti-nuke and anti-war demonstrations I joined, where people circulated legal-size, single-spaced printed sheets of information, and to the streets of Boston where I first heard about the coalition to stop violence against women, I had been reaching to place my hands upon that canvas, and it was there that, organizing with other Latinas, I learned about the work of activists of color, among them, that of Barbara Smith in women's studies.

The way I placed my own hands on the canvas was the equivalent of creating independent digital media in this century. It was done by creating poetry chapbooks to be sold (or, given away) at community bookstores; by creating posters that spelled out our names; by broadcasting in Spanish from WHUS, in Storrs; by creating a Latina lesbian newsletter in Somerville, Massachusetts; by contributing articles to journals; and, eventually, by joining Kitchen Table: Women of Color Press, in 1981, and eventually moving to New York City. But to get there, we have to imagine the many meetings in which we had been anonymous, the kind of *being*, the kind of person that the late María Lugones called *opaque* because our culture falls outside of what everyone seems to see so clearly: the transparent, the mainstream, where "only the culture of people who are culturally transparent is worth knowing."[6] We have to remember the meetings of the late '70s and the early '80s, when things began to look a bit different, to sound a bit different, and where, suddenly, there would be five Black women present! Two Latinas! One Asian! One Native American! Suddenly, upon that canvas of memory, there was the moment when I learned about *Conditions*. It was another meeting, another planning session for another event. At the end, Barbara Smith stood up, holding a book in her hands.

"I'd like to make an announcement," she said, "about *Conditions: Five*, the Black women's issue. . ." and her voice rose slightly at the end, as if *Conditions* might have been a book everyone had

---

6 María Lugones. "Purity, Impurity, and Separation." *Signs* 19, no. 2 (1994): 458–79.

heard about, and not the first of its kind. "But, just in case," she continued, "it's for sale at WomanBooks, for $3.00 each, and you can subscribe for $6.50 a year."

That was one of the moments when one wonders if things are about to change. In between protest marches and the production of art and literature, all you can do at that moment is hope, just the way communities are doing now, remembering Eleanor Bumpurs, and Eric Garner, and George Floyd, and Tony McDade, and Nina Pop, and Breonna Taylor, because gradually, quietly at first and then with fury, the canvas *has* changed, and you begin to recognize your life upon it. And, that journal that used to sell for $3.00 an issue, *Conditions*—"a magazine of writing by women with an emphasis on writing by lesbians"—that journal was there, at that beginning.

In order to write the story of how one particular journal, albeit a unique and hugely influential journal, transformed itself from a local literary production to one that would reach for a global perspective, it has been necessary to explain why the book with all its pages is important, but also why the work of the editors was so significant. The editors of *Conditions* were writers, and writers write, writers enunciate selves, and the language they use is of paramount importance in what becomes of the book that has been produced. Will it continue to be the organic, living thing that was created, as it passes from hand to hand? And, perhaps more urgently, does it matter today? In this essay, I am trying to propose an affirmative answer to that question.

I believe that the books we produced then mattered and continue to be living things—even as people search for them today and find them in digital form—because each book is a sort of protest against a void, against an existence of words and concepts that were not there before. I am relying on my own experience to reject the idea that a book is an object that remains static in an archive. When the editors of *Conditions* changed the nature of the journal by changing its focus, they allowed themselves to be transformed. Their position upon that that historical canvas had shifted. When they produced issue *Thirteen*, they let go of the book as object and allowed it to be a place of meeting. So, too, when they produced issue *Fourteen*, the use of Spanish appearing side by side with the English translation was further territory for the book to reclaim, to reterritorialize.[7]

With *Conditions: Fourteen* we can trace a more immediate expansion of meaning. There are so many ways to read the signifiers of the words written in the simple convention of listing contents that this exercise can be as conscious of its multiplicity and hybridity of form today as it was in 1987. A table of contents usually divides contents into sections by genre, an organization of texts that is the task of the editors, and one that can often be difficult and revealing at once. Even then, thirty-three years ago, genre was becoming fluid.

The first section is not labeled or subtitled in any way, and it is only when one opens the first section that the difficulty becomes apparent: the international focus of the issue is announced by the emphasis on the conditions of a diaspora, of Afro-German women who identify themselves and their experience. A photograph titled "Masai woman—Kenya," by Annette Peláez, a collective member, introduces the section. On the next page, above an excerpt of Audre Lorde's forthcoming book *A Burst of Light*, there is a content-theme subtitle that explains what we have here: "Promise of the Diaspora: Afro-German Women." Lorde's piece consists of two brief entries from 1984 in which she ponders the connection between Afro-German and African American women. The next entry is a poem titled "Afro-German," by May Opitz, followed by an excerpt of a dialogue between two sisters of Cameroonian and Prussian descent, Frieda and Anna. Both entries are reprinted from other journals and are translated by Ilze Mueller.

---

7 Gilles Deleuze and Félix Guattari, *A Thousand Plateaus: Capitalism and Schizophrenia* (Minneapolis: University of Minnesota Press, 1987).

The following sections of the issue are titled simply Fiction, Interview, Reviews, Essays, and Poetry, and each is introduced by a visual entry. We have another photograph by Annette Peláez, two photos by Margaret Randall, and a drawing by the artist Turtle-Bear. In each section, the intention to create an issue with an international focus on feminisms becomes apparent from the names of the authors as well as the topics covered, and though the distribution is not methodical or exhaustive, the overall effect demonstrates the care of the editors to reach out to writers whose subject would address international interests. In addition to Lorde's introduction to Afro-German women, there is a short story by Filipina poet and activist Mila D. Aguilar and a story by US-based Dominican writer Julia Álvarez. There is, as well, work by US-based fiction writers and poets, among them Leslea Newman, Valerie Miner, Chrystos, Jacqueline Lapidus (also translating from Portuguese), and Cheryl Clarke. Additionally, there are two interviews, with Puerto Rican–Dominican poet Sandra María Esteves, born in the Bronx, and Puerto Rican poet and academic Luz María Umpierre, born in Santurce, Puerto Rico.

Naturally, given that the issue contains several translations of seven poets publishing in Spanish, the poetry section is where we see the greatest variety simply in linguistic terms: there are poets from Cuba, El Salvador, and Costa Rica, and translators from Chile, Latvia, and the US. Yet it is important not to reduce national origin, language, and experience into markers for what constitutes the work of a multiracial and multinational group of writers and editors creating a diverse literary space. The various ways that we can read this book—by paying attention to the distribution of the material, the positioning of names and titles, front matter, writer bios, visual art, even the ads at the end of the issue (yes, there used to be ads that helped pay for the production of the journal)—all contribute to how we read the lives of writers with the added element of time.

In the layout of this last section, "Poetry," what emerges is a content listing that does not distinguish between poets whose work would not likely be found in an English language journal published in the US and those whose appearance in an anthology of this type, an independent feminist literary publication, would be expected. I have saved this aspect of my commentary for the end, because the ultimate effect of the compilation is the most important: it succeeds in breaking down a barrier, an implicit and artificial barrier that crumbles when it is not supported. The listing is not alphabetical, and it is not grouped according to language, but rather by a loose grouping of the Central American poets translated by Zoë Anglesey: Naranjo, Rodas, Avila, Martínez, and Istarú. Interspersed are the poets writing in English: Chrystos is the first poet, followed by Dorothy Randall Gray, and then by Cheryl Clarke and five other poets writing in English, including Margaret Randall. The listing ends with the two Cuban poets, Salado and Yáñez.

Reading according to the order of the table of contents, then, the texts seem to be elements of the book that find a place and accommodate where they are best suited to carry meaning and context rather than categorizing the authors, and this is perhaps a truer reflection of the work, political and literary, that was taking place across the globe at the time. *Conditions* represents the trajectory echoed by publications in many languages, starting from a void, from a place of non-existence and no-voice, to make room, to create space, and to legitimize thought and voices. On a parallel journey with publications like *Manushi*, published in India in 1978, and the long tradition of artisanal newsletters from Latin America since the 1930s, even the zines made by hand out of cardboard, by Eloísa Cartonera among others, the journals that were able to transform themselves—as their editors and writers transformed the world—interestingly had for the most part a limited run of a few years, at most one or two decades. That they were short-lived is beside the point; rather, it is the righteous upheaval they managed to create that matters.

I have chosen to focus on the particular moment in time when *Conditions* experienced a change in perspective because this was a type of righteous upheaval created beyond the margins. That *Conditions* and other publications developed in the territory of such margins is a given. More than that, it is a necessity for the social, political, and artistic margins to be actively engaged in cultural resistance against the mainstream in order for independent initiatives to create foundations of struggle against oppressions. Then transformation can occur aided by the conscious intention to change, as the international issues have done within the framework of the *Conditions* journal. These moments represent a halt, a rip in the fabric, a breach in the accepted and progressive politics, which is why they may be imperceptible—enunciations that take place at the interstice that is created beyond the margins, beyond the vanguards, and only at that particular time. This is a key aspect of the valuable contribution of *Conditions* to lesbian-feminist letters in the late twentieth century.

Mariana Romo-Carmona, Nuyorquina, born in Chile, has taught creative writing, Spanish, and comparative literature for many years, including at CUNY Colleges and the Goddard College MFA program. She has a PhD in Latin American, Iberian, and Latinx culture, and she currently teaches in the Latin American & Latinx Studies Program at the City College of New York. She is the author of *Living at Night*, *Speaking Like an Immigrant*, *Sobrevivir y otros complejos*, and *Conversaciones*. A longtime activist on the Latinx and queer fronts, she was an editor with Kitchen Table Press and *Conditions*. She co-edited *Cuentos: Stories by Latinas* and co-founded *COLORLife! Magazine* and Escritorial Press.

REWRITING OUR PAGES

Jewelle Gomez

When I left home—Boston—after undergraduate school in 1971, I was mostly alone in New York City, and for a time unemployed. The City felt as magical as I'd imagined it would, but I seemed to be watching the excitement through a window from somewhere outside. Eventually I developed some wonderful friends and even did freelance work for a couple of television news shows and film projects. While I was in grad school studying journalism, I also taught at a dynamic arts center in Westchester. So, I could say my life was full. Yet I felt I was still a bit on the margins.

I finally realized that when I left Boston, I'd also left behind my first and only lover: a girlfriend I'd had for four years (before she married a man). So, even with friends, I was alone in a profound way I hadn't been able to articulate. I was in a town where the gay hotline had no idea where the Black lesbian organization Salsa Soul Sisters met. Yet I knew there were other lesbians out there . . . . somewhere.

I understood I wasn't just looking for a new girlfriend; I was looking for a community of lesbians so I could feel at home again. When I moved into a flat that was a block from WomanBooks (on the Upper West Side of Manhattan), it was a lifesaver. I was shy but I went there for readings or browsing, often enough for the owner, Karyn, to learn my name and agree to carry my self-published poetry chapbook. She later invited me to join the team of poets—Marilyn Hacker and Sharon Olds—who programmed the bookstore's regular poetry reading series.

Being asked to work with those two notable writers was the equivalent (for me) of being invited to join the Nobel Prize Committee or the front bench of the Boston Celtics. I learned the names and the work of contemporary women writers and also came to know the audience for poetry. It was on the shelf at WomanBooks that I first saw *Conditions* magazine.

Conditions published its groundbreaking issue, *Conditions: Five / The Black Women's Issue*, which was guest-edited by Lorraine Bethel and Barbara Smith, in 1979. It was an impressive collection of writing by Black (mostly) lesbians. I'd only been living in NYC for eight years, but it felt like an eternity. I'd been writing poetry and had self-published my own first collection, so I snapped up the literary journal immediately. I was excited and proud to see so much work by those women. And I again felt like I was watching something wonderful happening from somewhere outside.

I imagine it was my work with WomanBooks that brought me to the attention of the editorial collective that produced *Conditions*. The founding collective, Elly Bulkin, Jan Clausen, Irena Klepfisz, and Rima Shore, decided at some point before or after *Conditions: Five* to expand the group. So they invited a new group of lesbians to join the collective and broaden the kinds of voices in their pages.

I was already devoted to the poetry of Irena Klepfisz, so I felt like I'd hit a second literary jackpot when I was invited to attend a meeting to meet the original editors and others who were potentially joining the collective. On the morning of the meeting I was extremely nervous for several reasons: first, I was taking a subway train to Brooklyn! I was still a small-town girl who marveled that I'd lasted in Manhattan as long as I had.

Another reason was that the editorial collective was all white. Even though I enjoyed the magazine, I imagined carefully coiffed, sophisticated New Yorkers wearing all black and with huge vocabularies. It was not an easy time in New York City for race relations—economics were bad, and Northern Black communities often felt as segregated as those in the South. I worked in the business world, so being the "colored one" among others was not an unusual circumstance. But an additional anxiety was that these women were EDITORS! For a nascent writer, that spelled terror.

All the reasons I might feel inadequate seemed to be printed on my forehead in an essay that they could magically correct with a red pen without me even opening my mouth.

Then there was the fact this was a Sunday afternoon gathering with a group of women who were total strangers. Worst date ever! It was like going to a cocktail party not knowing a soul in the room—and there would be no cocktails. I remember taking a deep breath before I entered the flat of fiction writer Dorothy Allison, a white Southern lesbian who was also new to the collective.

I was still a profound New Englander: what would I have to say to a white Southerner? It was like the setup for a bad joke or a bad racial incident.

I tamped down my fear and chose to focus on the fact that I was sitting in a room full of lesbians, something I'd been hoping desperately for since I'd arrived in New York City. And not just random lesbians, but lesbians who, like me, were enthusiasts of women's liberation and writing. I don't remember the format of that first meeting or who was there aside from Dorothy (maybe six newbies and the original editors). I do, of course, remember the poet Cheryl Clarke. I also remember that without much prompting, we all tumbled over each other's words to talk eagerly about books, poems, and stories we wanted to hear.

Adding to the collective was a bold political move on the part of the founding editors: *Conditions* was their baby, a successful lesbian literary journal thriving among the proliferation of women's publications at the height of the Women in Print Movement of the 1970s and '80s. A publication created and nurtured by two white lesbian couples provided it (I imagine this now but didn't think about it at the time) with a kind of continuity that can only be appreciated by those who have edited and published a journal.

That three of the four women were Jewish may have also infused the project with an early sense of stability that a disparate group would have had to work hard to create. Again, I'm guessing; we didn't know each other well enough yet to have that conversation. However, the ethnic connection made it feel to me more like marrying into a family than just joining an editorial collective. I don't know if they ever worried about how their readership would respond to this expansion. As we settled in, what I remember feeling was the editors' commitment to making us feel welcome and helping us understand the best ways to do the work, and their hope that we'd take ownership.

I also remember how much I learned from Elly Bulkin about editing and politics as she helped me edit the work of others, and later as she shaped my very first Gilda story. I was practically immobilized by stark terror the first time I talked with a writer about editing her work. In that session I learned as much about my own writing as I did about hers. Then there were the mechanics of literature. I'd never laid out a magazine before, so I was totally shocked to discover (this was pre-computers) we had to cut out the poems and stories and affix them to graph paper carefully, page by page. They were then, after checking and rechecking, sent to a printer . . . forever to hold our peace.

The experience was like taking a graduate course in lesbian literature. I came to know the work of writers such as Joy Harjo, Gloria Anzaldúa, Honor Moore, Paula Gunn Allen, and Mitsuye Yamada and developed relationships with many of them. Being in the *Conditions* collective led to my being asked to write a piece for the anthology *Home Girls*, as well as my developing friendships with Audre Lorde and Barbara Smith, and with writer Randye Lordon who came to *Conditions* after I left. It was as if the collective created a family that crossed time and was always connected.

My one regret was that my tenure with the magazine was short. I finally got a job, at the New York State Council on the Arts—which was one of the funders of the journal. After waiting so long, I was going to have to abandon the lively room full of lesbian literary feminists. We all agreed it was helpful to have me as an ally in the funding process, so I resigned to avoid a conflict of interest.

I was extremely sad to leave the collective but so proud when their application was brought up for discussion in the funding process.

Cheryl Clarke and Dorothy Allison eventually became two of my closest friends. Dorothy and I have since laughed often about that first meeting. Dorothy was nervous about the dreadlocked, serious-faced colored "gal" (me) sitting on her couch and I couldn't take my eyes off the chains hanging as a curtain in the doorway to her living room. This moment could have been the punchline to the bad joke.

Instead it turned out to be the place where a door opened, and I found myself invited into a world I'd only glimpsed from afar. The delicate process of being part of a lesbian collective has remained with me through the years. Whenever I set out to do work in collaboration with others, I think of how we managed to exchange passionate ideas with a minimum of rancor. We spent hours, almost in silence, diligently gluing poems to faint blue-lined graph paper with the same affection as for the time spent talking and eating bagels. I'm proud of the marches, fundraisers, and readings in which we participated, giving us shared experiences out in world and further cementing our personal connections.

Whenever anti-feminists (or just people who think they're cool) make fun of collectives, encounter groups, potlucks, or white feminists, I'm unable to remain silent. The building blocks of community can be awkward or opaque, but the sincerity has to be respected. And even when white feminists (from my favorite, Alice Paul, to anyone today) are not successful at being totally open or unbiased, feminism still remains the only political movement to articulate racial and gender equality as an inherent goal.

Almost forty years later, I value that sense of community and the political perspective on equality I came to understand while working on the *Conditions* collective. It replicated an earlier moment in the 1960s when I worked for an all-Black television show at WGBH in Boston. Both experiences confirmed the vision most progressive activists have: creating a world where each person feels like they belong and everyone is responsible for one another is a worthy goal.

The recent eruption of anger following the devastating barrage of police attacks and killings in black communities has sparked another movement to change the course of history and the shape of our culture. The lingering COVID-19 pandemic has also further nudged us toward change. The failure of government officeholders to support our democratic institutions has left the sick and dying by the side of the road. This could be a moment as ripe for reformation as this country was following the Civil War.

There was a lesson in learning how to build a magazine piece by patient piece: integrity and spatial relationships were as significant then as they are today. We're still working on social change in methodical, enduring ways. It remains to be seen if the pages can be rewritten and a new world can be built.

Jewelle Gomez is the author of the double Lambda Literary award–winning novel *The Gilda Stories* as well as the playwright-in-residence at New Conservatory Theatre Center, which has produced her work about James Baldwin, "Waiting for Giovanni," and her play about Alberta Hunter, "Leaving the Blues." @ VampyreVamp

WORKING ON A REVOLUTION . . .

Dorothy Allison

When the first evacuation order came in, we started packing the truck and my car with what we imagined might be necessities if we wound up somewhere south in some shelter, or more likely in a parking lot at a WalMart or a Target store. Notebooks, coffee, blankets, a bag of clothes, and yes, a box of books and notebooks with some flashlights tucked in between the paperbacks—everything was jumbled and confused. We were jumbled and confused, and exhausted. We had been watching the news and we knew how bad things were. But what do you do with a lifetime of stuff—mostly books and paper? I stood in my office and despaired. How could I leave all this behind to burn up and disappear? Full sets of feminist and lesbian journals, old issues of *Outlook* and all those unfinished manuscripts in the filing cabinets to the right of my desk? I had a brief flash of *Fahrenheit 451* and could not help but laugh. I should have memorized more poetry.

In the box of journals there were copies of both *Conditions* and *Sinister Wisdom*—random copies that for some reason had been near my desk. Pulling out a blank notebook, I looked at the spines of the *Conditions* and fell back forty years. Memory is a wedge not a bridge. It chops up events and people and resettles them in new shapes.

What did I think of when I remembered going to the meeting that invited us to join the collective staff of the established lesbian-feminist journal in that Brooklyn apartment?

Bagels and coffee and people's faces as carefully guarded as my own. We were all writers and some of us had met before. We knew each other vaguely, as we knew the original editors. Elly Bulkin caught my glance and nodded. She had come to a reading I had done over in Manhattan and we had spoken briefly. I was in awe of her and slightly terrified whether I was smart enough to match her intensity. Then there was Jewelle Gomez, whose poems I had read. She too was terrifying until she began to speak, and I fell half in love with her lyrical voice and her plainspoken willingness to talk about complicated issues. Each and every woman there seemed to join this pantheon in my mind of the best and strongest voices in lesbian feminism—and we were all being matched to each other in some astonishing decision by the staff that was retiring. Even scared shitless, I knew I was falling in love—not so much with the individual women, but with the intelligence and purpose I saw in those faces.

That was a good thing, because the next few years those women and that journal would take over my life.

I had a clerical job in Manhattan and took the subway back and forth, so I started collecting the mail for the magazine—piles of stories and letters and, more astonishingly, books. Review copies of books I could not afford to buy. A treasure, a bounty, a wonder. I read till my eyes blurred and had to learn to talk intelligently about what I read. You could not fake it at editorial meetings. You had to tell the truth, say this is better than that. That was a challenge for me since I was still in the glory period of believing that every woman's story was vital. But then I had to admit that it was sometimes hard to even understand what one woman or another was saying in that poem or story. I had to surrender to the notion that, yes, all women's voices were important, but some could tell a story in a way that pulled you in, and some could not. We all took our positions as editors seriously, so we trained ourselves—each other—to make judgments and choose this piece, but not that one. Or to seek out and work with the writer to make the piece better.

But oh! Those editorial meetings!

Sitting on the floor of my big old half-empty apartment in Brooklyn with stacks and stacks of paper and books and arguing fiercely while eating bagels or carrots or pastries.

"No, no. Listen to this. Hear how she does this! It's wonderful!"

"It's self-righteous twaddle!"

"It's incomprehensible."

"It's glorious, read it again."

An education I sometimes wanted to resist took place in those meetings. I think I finally began to grow up there . . . except the life I was actually living complicated everything.

That day job in Midtown Manhattan was killing me. I found myself replacing the woman who had been running the information center at Poets & Writers just about the time I started trying to publish some of my awful poetry and stories. I was also trying to complete a masters in anthropology at the New School, where one professor joked that I could provide both the feminist and "peasant" perspectives. I was too scared to say much in response though I knew he was a fool. But I had no confidence in much of anything I could actually do. I felt like I was faking it all the time, just showing up at the office or the college and certainly at the collective meetings for *Conditions*.

How can I explain how I managed?

How did I keep writing when I could see my writing was not as good as the stories we were reading for the magazine?

"You're getting better," a girlfriend told me, but I didn't much trust her.

I didn't much trust anybody—and I had reason for that, big complicated reasons.

At those editorial meetings on the rug-covered hardwood floors, I would shift and try not to groan. I was black and blue from thighs to shoulders and carefully dressed to disguise that fact. After those long hard days at the office or the school, I would take a subway out to Queens to spend the night with the two women who gave me those bruises, and the orgasms that drove me nearly out of my mind. They were a butch-femme couple with skills and equipment, and stamina enough even for my outrageous desires. In the grip of their hands I felt almost sane. But none of it was explainable. Sex. It fueled me and made sense on a level I could not explain, though it seemed to me that everyone I knew acted on desire more often than they would acknowledge and I was convinced that feminism at its most basic level celebrated and honored women's desire. A lesbian-feminist ecology of lust was shaping up in my imagination, but I was sure that almost everything I believed about living as a lesbian was shared among us who were struggling to build a society that acknowledged and honored our most secret desires. It was just that my desires were somehow secret even from myself. How to explain a lesbian-feminist who needed to be hurt just to come to orgasm?

"You're just a garden-variety masochist," one of girlfriends told me. "Somebody kicks you around a bit and fucks you right, and you will fall all over yourself to come back for more."

She was right, of course, about the masochism. I could not deny that, except as I rejected any notion that I was "garden-variety." I was exceptional, goddamn it. Yes, I had been regularly beaten and raped as a child. Yes, something in me had fought back by feeling heroic for surviving that with any sense of self at all. Along the way all my desires were bent toward a recreation of that heroism. I am who I am, I told myself, and to hell with anyone who cannot understand the complications of it.

Pity, it was not so simple. The fact was, I was also deeply ashamed of my own desires, my need to orgasm in hands that bruised and pummeled. Even as I was determined not to be the creature my stepfather had tried to make me, I sought out women who were rougher than he had ever been. It was unexplainable to people who would look at me with pity and contempt for the ways I tried to work my way to a sense of self that needed teeth and muscle to feel desire. I had to have clenched muscles and screams to reach the release that left me sweaty and weak and completely satisfied. I knew that. It was simple. Surely that was not so hard to understand. Many women shared those issues with me. How could we accept an ideology that required us to forgo what we needed to reach our own satisfaction? Who the hell thought it was reasonable to tell us to wait till after the revolution to have satisfying relations?

Yes, yes, I could think that way and shape arguments that supported what I did just to collapse satisfied in bedsheets tangled with sweat and struggle. The problem was that all my notions of women's courage and strength and independence were ways to fight being the animal I did not want to be. No, the animal I knew I was. Maybe I was a kind of monster—a broken stubborn girl who had found power in endurance and satisfaction in acts I did not want to describe to the virginal open-faced glances of respectable lesbians. But if I was going to acknowledge myself a monster, then I was going to be a monster with ethics and conviction. I was going to work to try and shape a world where girls would not be broken on the wheel of men's violence. But also a world in which broken girls (and I counted myself one) could mend themselves in communities of outlaw conviction. *This is what I do to get myself off. What do you do?* I wanted to help shape a community where we could say any of that without fear. I suspected it might take years to get anywhere near such a notion—and I was right. Meanwhile I had work to do. We all had.

Sitting on the floor at editorial meetings talking about writing and manuscripts and how women might work toward a more just and equitable world, I looked around and felt my heart thudding behind my breasts. I loved each and every one of us. I loved what we were trying to do even as we quibbled over line breaks in a poem or structure in an essay. I loved it when one of us would champion a story even as we acknowledged its flaws.

"I'll talk to her," I'd say, and see Jewelle nod. Then she would take a dozen poems and work through them to find the strongest to defend, and say that she would write the poet and get her to let us just use the best.

Meetings and meetings, days and days, months on months, and issue by issue, the work was relentless, demanding, and the best of all the things I wanted to do. Still it is impossible to explain how balanced my complicated, unbalanced life was. I found love, acceptance, and purpose in working on writing with those extraordinary women while keeping my wild adventures with dark-eyed dangerous lovers unspoken, or mentioned only briefly and with no emphasis. I worked hard as an organizer and an editor with the journal, while working equally hard to form an organization and an alliance for lesbians like me who treated sexual adventure as an outlaw vindication, a source of power and energy that was almost unexplainable to the feminists I worked with every day.

There was something inherently banal about the work of publishing a feminist magazine—all that proofreading and editorial notes, and talking to young writers who were deeply flattered that I admired their work, but ready to argue me to a draw about sentence structure and word choices. At the same time there was an enormously satisfying accomplishment in doing something so private and everyday as writing a story or helping someone else write a story while believing yourself a revolutionary on the front lines of struggle.

What lay behind those years of hard work and exhaustion were the relationships we developed arguing story and rhyme and feminist ethics and structure. I fell in love with us—us different, determined lesbians trying to build the just society we all wanted. That we had different notions of what that might look like made perfect sense to me, for as much as we valued and admired each other, I knew we were also uncertain about each other and sometimes downright scared or angry as we tried to work together. I was poor white trash from South Carolina with a half-completed degree in anthropology that made me think I was smarter than I was, and a secret, desperate passion to write all the stories that echoed in my back brain. And I knew myself a complete pervert, a masochist who tried to be matter-of-fact about the nature of my sexuality, but found ways to avoid much in the way of details about how that functioned for me. No matter that I was also working with

Black women, Yankee women, and women who had been feminist activists while I was hanging out in bars flirting with half-drunk angry butches who would drag me in the bathroom and talk dirty to me. In editorial meetings we were careful with each other, which is to say we knew who we were, and we could call out each other on our differences while still trying to get the work done. Bottom line was that I knew I had been raised to be a racist and to hate people who had more than my family did and god knows we had damn little, so the list of people I feared and resented was enormous. But I was also trying hard to understand my own prejudices and fears and shake them off—to say, "I don't understand" or "I need to think about that" and see if I could not change. I could stand in the apartments of the other editors and see the huge gulf in our life experiences and access to resources—the beautiful furniture; real bookcases, not assemblages of board and bricks; and clothes bought new, not acquired in thrift stores. I would listen to them talk and make notes of books they mentioned that I was going to have to run out and read. Desperate, competitive, and terrified I was not smart enough or sensitive enough to be worth anyone's trust, I continually took deep breaths and made my back muscles relax. I listened and made notes and thought long and hard. I made myself trust what I feared could not be trusted—both myself and those women across the stacks of paper and books.

The result was simple. I made deep friendships and powerful alliances. Together we produced a body of work I treasure, years of journals that still stand as the best evidence of what lesbian-feminist writing and thought could produce. We led huge, complicated lives and defended each other whenever any of us needed the understanding and commitment we honed on hardwood floors across platters of bagels. I am proud of every moment I spent in that communion.

I am seventy-one now and I can look back at those years with sharper eyes than I want to explain. Much has changed, though the world is still as big and mean as it ever was, and the challenges we face ever more complicated. I have worked myself to an acceptance of what I have managed and what I have not. I have written books I am proud of, though never as many as I planned. I read the books, plays, and poems we have all produced with awe and love and pride. If Jewelle or Cheryl or Elly or any of the many women I worked with in those years calls me up and asks me for anything, I find a way to get back to them. The unfolding, unfinished work goes on.

I can live with that, but right now I have to take another look at my books and papers and repack the car. Another heat wave is said to be coming this next week and with it the risk of more fires. I seem to have chosen a foolish place to plant my family life— here in the midst of a redwood forest threatened by fire. For years we have organized our life here to get through flood season, to be cut off without power and read novels by lantern light. Floods seem almost reasonable to me now. Fire gives no quarter. All the tangible evidence of years of work and care can be stolen by one strong hot wind. It is memory that survives even as it grows more fragile and untrustworthy. But then of course there is story. I believe in story, the human need to explain or examine or just recount what happened, might have happened or should have happened, or even still might happen.

We did that, do that, hope for that.

Dorothy Allison, now in her seventies, remains a stubborn lesbian writer and activist. Her books include *Bastard Out of Carolina*, *Trash*, *Two or Three Things I Know for Sure*, *Skin*, and *Cavedweller*. She has a vast archive of photographs, books, journals, and ephemera from other lesbian writers and activists that help keep her relatively sane.

INTENTIONAL LESBIAN EXPERIENCE
Cheryl Clarke

As Black feminists and Lesbians we know that we have a very definite revolutionary task to perform and *we are ready for the lifetime of work and struggle before us.*
—"The Combahee River Collective Statement," Boston, 1977 (italics mine)

As a thirty-four-year-old arrogant dyke-trying-to-be-poet, I already had been published in three now-iconic, then "famous" lesbian feminist publications: *Conditions: ¹Five, The Black Women's Issue* (1979), edited by Barbara Smith and Lorraine Bethel; n's *Lesbian Poetry* edited by Elly Bulkin's *Lesbian Poetry* and Joan Larkin; and *This Bridge Called My Back: Writings by Radical Women of Color,* edited by Cherríe Moraga and the late Gloria Anzaldúa. These publications explain why I was arrogant. Barbara Smith, whom I had met in 1975, recommended me to the *Conditions* Collective at the time three of the four founding editors—Rima Shore, Elly Bulkin, Jan Clausen—were reaching out to create a more racially, regionally, and class diverse editorial collective membership. I was invited to join in 1981. *Conditions,* "a magazine of writing by women with an emphasis on writing by lesbians," was just what I needed. And of most importance to me was the enouncement by the founding editors to produce a

---

1 In 1973, Assata Shakur (nee Joanne Chesimard) was riding in a car with two other passengers, Zayd Shakur and Sundiata Acoli. They were stopped by the N.J. State Troopers on the New Jersey Turnpike allegedly for a defective revolutionary Black Liberation Army and Werner Foerster, a N.J. State Trooper were killed. Sundiata and Assata were jailed, tried, and convicted, in separate trials, in New Brunswick. Sundiata was convicted of the Murder of Werner Foerster in 1973. Assata was convicted in 1976 as an accomplice to Foerster's murder. She escaped from Clinton Prison in 1979. Sundiata is still serving time.

magazine that speaks to women for whom a commitment to women is integral to their lives. This was a brilliant assertion.

I had burnt myself out on the New Jersey Defense Committee for Assata Shakur. Assata was jailed and ultimately tried and convicted of murder in New Brunswick, N.J. between 1973 and 1976. During those years, the Committee's work called for going to court during Assata's trial, leafleting the train and bus stations in New Brunswick, and building support for her case and cause locally. She *made* her own freedom circa 1978 and didn't need the foot-soldiers any longer, (except for that last foot soldier who got her to the underground to Havana.)

In the middle of my Assata work, I attended the exceedingly lesbian-phobic Socialist Feminist Conference in Yellow Springs, Ohio—the same one mentioned in the famous "Combahee Statement"—in 1975. There I first met Barbara Smith and for the first time saw the legendary Charlotte Bunche in the flesh; Charlotte tried valiantly to explain the political insights lesbians bring to feminism and socialism, but the socialist feminists were not having it. Homophobia was rampant, as were the lesbians, (out and closeted) there at the conference.

Circa 1977-'80, the "Black Feminist Retreats," on the East Coast, organized by Barbara Smith, were life-changing and transformative for me. The twelve to 20 of us who attended came from California, Chicago, New York, New Jersey, Massachusetts, Connecticut, Delaware. At an early Retreat Barbara and Demita Frazier introduced the "Combahee Statement," to one of its first live audiences—the twelve to 20 of us. (Zillah Eisenstein's *Capitalist Patriarchy and the Case for Socialist Feminism* [(1978] had accepted the "Statement" for publication.) There, in those intellectual, emotive, *politic* spaces, we defined a way to change ourselves and the world with black women at the center. We sustained ourselves through networks of feminists, locally and globally. Like *Conditions*, the Black Feminist Retreats emphasized lesbians, if my memory serves me.

As I am about to look back almost forty years to my editorial beginnings with *Conditions* ("the magazine"), I did not have enough foresight, then, to look to the "lifetime of work and struggle," quoted above. So, even before the first Black Feminist Retreats, I knew I had to live according to lesbian-feminist values, endlessly trying to integrate the ever-elusive race, sex, and class politics. Each always clamoring to be singular.

I accepted the invitation to join. *Conditions* was for me a defining moment. I had to learn new politics, new skills, new competencies to turn out annually the premiere lesbian-feminist journal *Conditions* was. Actually, as Irena Klepfisz had said, "It's really an anthology." We casually referred to it as "the magazine," which featured the work of women writing for their and our lives and our art. I *learned* from the three founding editors, Elly Bulkin, Jan Clausen, and Rima Shore,[2] who did not suffer fools gladly. Good thing I wasn't a fool. I had a lot to learn. So did they. When I first joined, the other new editors were the late Carroll Oliver, Dorothy Allison, Jewelle Gomez, Mirtha Quintanales. Cherríe Moraga was our office manager. I couldn't look at my own writing or *my own self* the same again; nor anyone else's writing that I would ever read. A life changing-never-been-the-same-since experience. The exponential impact of 3,000 books a year, whether subscriptions or distribution in bookstores, academic institutions, prisons, mental institutions, at public events, cannot be "gainsaid," as my friend, the late Cheryl Wall said in 1989 of black women writers.

Conditions was my first all-lesbian experience. I would like to use the term "facilitation," instead of "leadership," to identify assertive actions that involve consensus and movement toward a certain result. As editors, practicing publishing, we attempted an integrated politics à la Combahee. By then, many white lesbian-feminist organizations were emulating the *Conditions* model. Women of color organizations were working to mediate

---

2 Irena Klepfisz had already left the magazine by the time I joined.

our multi-faceted cultural identifications, as they converged in our practice. Commitment to women of color facilitation was principal to our practice. To "know there is such a thing as racial-sexual oppression, which is neither solely racial nor solely sexual" ("Combahee"), and to assiduously "band together" with others to do, as we now call it, our "intersectional" political work were imperative. To be nonjudgmental—the most difficult to achieve. Once achieved, how practiced.

Continuing to justify the "all-lesbian" collective became more complicated as the decade of the 1980s rolled on to an end, however. "There are women, not identified as lesbians, who would join and help us stay viable as a publication. Let's be practical instead of separatist," one editor admonished us (mainly me) many times. As committed as I am to an integrated struggle, I am still committed to autonomy—of lesbian-identified and led organizations—and not separatism. Lesbian focus. Lesbians focus. The more lesbians, the more focus. And there is only so much time. Also, I was dedicated to the ideals of the founding editors—I sound like one of those appeals to "the founding fathers"—the all-lesbian collective.

During my years with the magazine, I worked with 20 different editors. I couldn't imagine producing *Conditions* with fewer than seven at any one time, though the founding editors did it with four. We were our only volunteers. We had several office managers—each of whom served us well, (including Chirlane McCray, New York City Mayor Bill de Blasio's wife now; but she was a lesbian then and a good office manager.) We had each other as editors and twice monthly meetings on Saturdays, in Park Slope mostly. New Brunswick, N.J., where I lived, was an hour from Manhattan. (Thanks to my dear parents, I had a car.) In addition to those mentioned above, my debt of gratitude goes out to: Mi Ok Bruining, Nancy Clarke Otter, Pam A. Parker, Annette Peláez, Mariana Romo Carmona (whose reflection is included here), Sabrina, Deb Schaubman, P. Mikie Sugino, and Adrienne Waddy.

And I also express my gratitude to the women who served as our office managers during my time: Cherrie Moraga, Shelley Messing, again Adrienne Waddy, and Chirlaine McCray.

Conditions: Eight (http://www.lesbianpoetryarchive.org/ node/325) broke me in. I remember Elly Bulkin's phone-call to me one Saturday, after I had missed several important production meetings for *Eight*. She called me and asked kindly, "Will you come to a meeting today?" I said yes. I drove in. And I said to Elly that day, when I got to the meeting: "I would give anything for *Conditions*." Elly retorted, "Come to meetings and do what you say you will do." *Do what you say you will do.*

Much as it is not my style to be autobiographical, I must say that *Conditions* made possible my five-year relationship with Jewelle L. Gomez. She left the Collective in 1982, because the New York State Council on the Arts (NYSCA), which funded *Conditions*, wisely employed her to work in its Literature Program with the late Gregory Kolovakis. Both Gregory and Jewelle ferried *Conditions* and many other progressive arts groups through years of funding cycles and defended us against attacks from conservative, homophobic, and right-wing legislators in New York and Washington, D.C.

Jewelle and I contributed to women of color lesbian literary culture. It shaped us and shapes us. We did our work. We lived together in Jersey City during those five years, in a very lovely apartment, a 1930's two-story Victorian. And we had good times, demanding full-time jobs, and hectic writing lives. The work of lesbian-feminism kept us traveling, driving, running—often together and often separately. Thank you, dear Jewelle, for our time together.

Just briefly, I want to signal some memorable aspects of production, for me, of *Conditions: Eight* through *Seventeen*. However, memory becomes difficult. *Conditions:Eight* broke me in and promised to report in *Conditions:Nine* on the Collective's process of transition, with its haunting Gwyn Metz cover photo of a black

"Girl Ice Skating." I made my editing debut in *Issue Nine*, one of the longer issues, with the controversial "Black Women On Black Women Writers" or what we came to call the "pentalog: a conversation of five [black feminists]" which appeared on its pages, with cover of a pin and ink drawing by Gaia. The red cover of *Ten*, designed by artist Anne Cammett, with "CONDITIONS" fading 10 times, announced the formidable writing within. *Conditions: 11/12 / The Double Issue*: with so many submissions, pressed us to produce a double issue. Same challenge with submissions as *Conditions:11/12*, but with a different decision: *Conditions: Thirteen / International Issue* I and *Conditions: Fourteen / International Issue II* compelled us to produce two volumes, with covers by artist Dorothy Randall Gray. Emboldened by our foray into the international forum, *Conditions:Fifteen* reaffirmed the magazine's wide lens. Our "greatest hits" issue, *Conditions: Sixteen / The Retrospective*, featured writers from *One* through *Fifteen*; and *Seventeen*, our final issue, graced our readers with editor Mariana Romo-Carmona's translations of poems by Japanese, Peruvian poet, Doris Moromisato. The artist Eve Sandler designed the covers for Issues *Fifteen*, *Sixteen* and *Seventeen*.

My co-editors Melinda Goodman, Paula Martinac, P. Mikie Sugino, Mariana, and I said the following to readers in our final "Introduction":

> We found that with full-time jobs and other community commitments, we could no longer devote ourselves to the work required to maintain *Conditions* as a yearly journal and as an organization; but we wanted to ensure that it would continue to exist as a source for new writing by women. *Conditions*, the anthology, will still publish the best new writing by women, with an emphasis on writing by lesbians. [And] we hope our readers will continue to support *Conditions* in its new format. (*Seventeen*, vi)

The Conditions "anthology . . . . in its new format" did not come to be for many reasons having to do with the fragility of women's independent publishing at the time. For me, I found the work gets too hard. Time gets too tight. Other demands persist and insist. The job, no car, no flow. The news of the ending of *Conditions* was not well-received by former editors and friends. Two former editors scolded me: "You should have raised the requisite funds to keep the magazine going." The editors, at the time, didn't like closing the covers of the magazine either, including me. Magazines don't last forever. Nor do editors. Nor does funding. And time gets too tight.

Sinister Wisdom, the longest-running lesbian journal in the world probably, is a year older than *Conditions* would have been, had it continued publishing. They were good friends, *Sinister Wisdom* and *Conditions*. *Sinister Wisdom*'s production of this special issue enlarges memory where it is inadequate and recovers it where it has been lost. *Conditions* leaves a radical legacy—in the sense Ella Baker meant *radical*—i.e., "tearing up from the root"— of lesbian literature, leadership, legibility, and multicultural commitments.

Conditions probed and pierced many ideas of women's sexuality and gender consciousness through many forms of writing by lesbians —this had not happened in print before by anybody, rilly. No. Pierced to the root and signified self-deter- mination—independence from and resistance against the (old) white male—heterosexual—literary mainstream canon. *Condi- tions* moved toward the integrated analysis and practice/praxis "Combahee" and other black feminist texts of the late seventies and early eighties called for: integration of writing forms and cultural, regional, class politics of writers and readers. *Conditions* ended because publications don't last and don't always have to last, though if they are righteous, we wish them to last beyond *last*. But we are nostalgic things, in the worst and better senses. We want them to last for our individual(istic) selves. Don't we?

Organizations, groups, collectives, whatever, don't last of themselves. We make them last. And when we cease to do the work to make organizations, groups, collectives, whatever, last, they crash, fold, become co-opted, or end. *Conditions* ended, with dignity. She had a good run, a really good run. And the "struggle" is still "before us."

Black lesbian feminist poet **Cheryl Clarke** has been involved with lesbian literary production since 1981, when she joined the *Conditions* magazine editorial collective. She remained a member until 1990, when the magazine shuttered. She is a member of the board of *Sinister Wisdom* and co-edited in 2018 *Dump Trump: Legacies of Resistance* (#110) with Morgan Gwenwald, Stevie Jones, and Red Washburn. *By My Precise Haircut* is her most recent book of poetry (The Word Works, 2016). She is a co-editor of this special issue on *Conditions*.

CONDITIONS, IKON, LONG HAUL PRESS
KITCHEN TABLE WOMEN OF COLOR PRESS, 13TH MOON

PRESENT

A SERIES OF
WOMEN READING

in conjunction with ARTISTS CALL Against U.S. Intervention in Central America

FEBRUARY 7
Elly Bulkin
Toi Derricotte
Marilyn Hacker
Barbara Smith

FEBRUARY 14
Cheryl Clarke
Jan Clausen
Kimiko Hahn
Mary Jane Sullivan

FEBRUARY 21
LATINA WRITERS
co-ordinated by
KITCHEN TABLE,
Women of Color Press
Gloria Anzaldúa
Alma Gómez
Mirtha Quintanales
Cherríe Moraga

FEBRUARY 28
Davine
Jewelle Gomez
Susan Sherman
Rima Shore

MARCH 6
Dorothy Allison
Patricia Jones
Chris Llewellyn
Marie Ponsot

TUESDAYS, 7:30 pm
CONTRIBUTION

CENTRAL HALL GALLERY
386 West Broadway, 4th Floor, 226-9215

RESPONSES
TO
CONDITIONS

CONDITIONS: ONE
— Response by Rachel Corbman

Historical *Conditions*: Movement Projects and Academic Precarity in the 1970s and 1980s

The feminist literary magazine *Conditions* is most often—and rightly—read as part of the history of the Women in Print Movement, one of many independently produced lesbian "books, chapbooks, journals, newspapers, and other printed materials" that proliferated in the 1970s and 1980s.[1] Perhaps surprisingly, though, *Conditions* also has a clear, if fraught, relationship to the political economy of US colleges and universities. In the pages that follow, I reflect on the academic lives of the four founders of *Conditions*, all of whom spent significant portions of their careers in non-tenure track positions in colleges and universities. In founding *Conditions*, they created an intellectual home for a cohort of lesbian writers who worked outside of the academy or in precarious relation to it. *Conditions* thus served as a crucial—if limited—strategy for cultivating a feminist and queer intellectual community at a time when a hefty proportion of academics were "kicked out the door" of colleges and universities.[2]

***

A decade before founding *Conditions* with Rima Shore and Jan Clausen, Irena Klepfisz and Elly Bulkin attended graduate school in

---

1 Julie R. Enszer, "Fighting to create and maintain our own Black women's culture': *Conditions* Magazine, 1977–1990," *American Periodicals*, 25.2 (2015), 160

2 Cassius Adair, Cameron Awkward-Rich, and Amy Marvin, "Before Trans Studies" *TSQ* 7.3 (2020), 315

the 1960s. Born in Poland in 1941, Klepfisz grew up in a working-class Jewish neighborhood in the Bronx. In 1963, she received a BA from the then–tuition free City College before moving to Chicago, where she completed a PhD in English at the University of Chicago in 1970. Four years younger than Klepfisz, Bulkin was born into a lower-middle-class Jewish family and received a PhD in American studies from New York University in 1973.

It is unlikely that women like Klepfisz and Bulkin would have entertained the idea of an academic job, which were historically reserved for privileged white men, if they had been born any earlier. Crucially, however, they arrived on campus, as undergraduate and graduate students, during the so-called "golden era" of higher education—a period of state-sponsored growth spurred on by educational benefits that the GI Bill afforded to primarily white male veterans of World War II, and an unprecedented level of federal spending on Cold War–related research. By the 1960s, colleges and universities also benefited from a surge in the enrollment of the baby boom generation. Increased undergraduate enrollment also encouraged the expansion of graduate education. For example, in 1964, the National Commission on the Humanities released a report on the state of the field that emphasized the need to fund graduate education in the humanities. Universities, the report reasoned, must respond to the "rapid increase in the number of college students" by subsidizing the recruitment of graduate students "to such an extent that we can attract into the profession the number and the quality that we need."[3] In the years that followed, universities slowly and unevenly began to fund graduate students in the humanities, eventually crystallizing into the new normal of guaranteeing incoming doctoral students a stipend for

3   National Commission on the Humanities, "Report of the Commission on the Humanities," (1964), p. 139 https://publications.acls.org/NEH/Report-of-the-Commission-on-the-Humanities-1964.pdf

a set number of years, often in exchange for part-time teaching.[4] Klepfisz and Bulkin were recipients of this mid-century largesse.

But despite the optimism of the 1960s, the academic job market shrank in the 1970s, following a global recession in 1973. Klepfisz and Bulkin thus entered the academic job market during what many diagnosed as an "overwhelming job crisis," which profoundly shaped the trajectories of new PhDs.[5] Bulkin, for example, initially secured a full-time lectureship on the Brooklyn campus of Long Island University. However, "after four years," her contract was not renewed, and she was left without work in what "had become a very tight academic job market."[6] Similarly, after finishing her PhD, Bulkin taught English as an adjunct at Borough of Manhattan Community College (BMCC).[7] Later, she found a non-faculty position as the assistant director of the Women's Center at Brooklyn College.

While Bulkin "threw herself" into her new position, Klepfisz initially struggled to imagine a life unbound from an imagined academic future.[8] For Klepfisz, academia initially seemed like a

---

4 I would be remiss not to mention that graduate stipends often fall below the standard of living. My point in tracing this longer history is not to undermine the efforts of graduate student organizers in demanding higher stipends. On the contrary, I believe the history of why universities began offering stipends in the first place is potentially helpful in shaping messaging for organizers in the present.

5 Sandy Cooper, "Women and the Historical Profession: Looking Ahead" report, November 1974, Berkshire Conference of Women Historians (MC 606), Box 15, Folder 3, Schlesinger Library, Cambridge, MA

6 Ginny Vida, *New Our Right to Love: A Lesbian Resource Book* (New York: Touchstone, 1996), p. 237

7 Bulkin discusses her experience teaching at Manhattan Community College in an interview with Adrienne Rich, which is printed in *Conditions: One.* See pages 58–9.

8 Jan Clausen, *Apples and Oranges* (Boston: Houghton Mifflin Company, 1999), p. 129. In her memoir, Clausen refers to Bulkin with a pseudonym, but biographical details do not appear to have been altered.

"way out" of the working class.[9] As a graduate student, her sense of herself as an academic also more generally structured her identity. "Most of my friends were academics," she told Ginny Vida in a 1996 interview. "We all defined ourselves by our work."[10] Ultimately, the growing lesbian-feminist movement offered Klepfisz a means of sustaining her sense of self as an intellectual outside of the academy, even as it did little to address her economic precarity. After coming out as a lesbian, Klepfisz joined the Brooklyn-based Seven World Poets, a writing support group for lesbians. Through the writing group, Klepfisz met Jan Clausen, a twenty-four-year-old college dropout who would later go on to teach writing at NYU, Eugene Lang, and Goddard College. At the time, Clausen and Bulkin were partners, while Klepfisz was dating Rima Shore, a doctoral student in Russian literature at Columbia University. In 1976, the two couples founded *Conditions* together.

Over the next fourteen years, *Conditions* served as an important venue for feminist and proto-queer thought, publishing, as Klepfisz puts it, "a lot of people who we now take for granted," but who were "just beginning their careers" in the late 1970s and early 1980s.[11] Barbara Smith, for example, published "Toward a Black Feminist Criticism" in the second issue of *Conditions*, an essay that Smith singles out as her "most immediately catalytic" and subsequently reprinted work.[12] Similarly, a decade before *Bastard Out of Carolina* (1992) catapulted her into the mainstream, much of Dorothy Allison's early fiction appeared in *Conditions*, including her semi-autobiographical stories "I Am Working on My Charm" and "My Career as a Thief." Cherríe Moraga's poems "Anatomy

---

9 Vida, *New Our Right to Love*, p. 238

10 Vida, *New Our Right to Love*, p. 238

11 Ibid.

12 Barbara Smith, *The Truth That Never Hurts* (New Brunswick, NJ: Rutgers University Press, 2000), 3

Lesson" and "For the Color of My Mother," likewise, were printed in *Conditions* in 1981, the same year that her important anthology with Gloria Anzaldúa, *This Bridge Called My Back: Writings of Radical Women of Color*, came out with Persephone Press. *Conditions* also published historian of science Evelynn Hammonds before she started her PhD at Harvard and queer theorist Judith Butler, back when she earnestly described herself as "a lesbian and aspiring philosopher since the early stages of youth" in her author bio.[13]

These now famous names might retroactively read like an odd mix of activists, popular writers, and academic "stars." However, they all shared space in a movement journal *and* worked in colleges and universities at some point in their career. Hammonds and Butler of course went on to hold tenured positions at major research universities. But the founders of *Conditions* and many of its storied contributors did not. Smith and Allison, for example, dropped out of PhD programs in the 1980s, and Moraga and Anzaldúa edited *This Bridge Called My Back* while working as lecturers in the Cal State system.[14] Eventually, Moraga landed a job on the strength of her literary career, first at Stanford and now at the University of California, Santa Barbara. Her co-editor and friend Anzaldúa, however, died at the age of sixty-one while still working as a lecturer at the University of California, Santa Cruz. The composite of these individual trajectories reveals a system in which there are multiple graduate school dropouts and academics in contingent positions for every success story. This phenomenon is not limited to feminist and queer thinkers and may not index all that much about women's, gender, and sexuality studies as a field, which has in fact expanded its foothold in the academy since the

---

13 Judith Butler's review of Marilyn Fyre's *The Politics of Reality* appears in *Conditions: Ten.* See page 180 for her biographical note.

14 Nick Mitchell, "Theses on Adjunctification," February 26, 2015 https://www.lowendtheory.org/post/112138864200/theses-on-adjunctification

institutionalization of the first women's studies programs in the 1970s. Rather, I see the scarcity of jobs as a more general feature of an academic job market that has been in nearly perpetual crisis since the mid-1970s.

Movement projects like *Conditions* were often ill-equipped to combat large-scale structural problems. However, these projects intervened on micropolitical scales. Specifically, *Conditions* opened up a space for a cohort of writers with various relationships to universities. These writers in turn bequeath a legacy of ideas dreamed up in the pages of *Conditions*, which now circulate on the Internet, in college classrooms, and through citational trails that weave their way through contemporary feminist and queer studies. But as well as reading *Conditions* as a product of a particular past, we can also read *Conditions* as a model for the sort of intellectual spaces we need to cultivate in the present, places where we can, as *Conditions* contributor Susan Krieger wrote, "make sense" of ourselves and "create livable worlds in writing."[15]

Rachel Corbman is a visiting assistant professor of women's, gender, and sexuality studies at Wake Forest University. She is currently working on "Conferencing on the Edge: A Queer History of Feminist Field Formation, 1969–1989," a book on the history of feminist and queer field formation. Her research has been published in journals such as *Feminist Formations, GLQ, Continuum,* and *Histoire Sociale / Social History.*

---

15   This quote is from Susan Krieger's bio in *Conditions: One.* See page 140 for her biographical note.

CONDITIONS: TWO
— Response by Shawn(ta) Smith-Cruz

A Kind of Wistfulness: Reflecting on my Saturn Return

At twenty-seven years old, I began having periodic dreams of my belly gravitating from my center, or ripped open, or growing, or shrinking. My mother would be nearby, but stationary at my doorway, drowning in her own tears of disappointment, the moisture pulling her down like lava-quicksand, her arms reaching to my large or ripped or absent belly, the sound of a wailing newborn, the world growing dark around me. Sometimes there were flames. I'd wake retching in fetal position, cradling my center, panting, or grabbing my pillow to prevent a great fall. It was the first time I felt an intense emptiness, the presence of an absence. I learned later that these dreams happened most often during ovulation. Otherwise, I'd wake to the baby's cries, which stopped short once I looked down at the blood-soiled sheets.

One autumn evening at the slowdown of a Brooklyn Black-dyke-dinner-party, prompted by the loud gurgling sound of suds absorbed by the kitchen sink's drain, I shared my dreams with the few women left standing. "Oh girl, you're twenty-seven! You're entering your Saturn Return, that's all," the host soothed, then handed me a book. Apparently, these would be the most tumultuous years of my life until I hit thirty or thirty-one, but by thirty-two, it would all plateau. I became obsessed with the Saturn Return: started a blog (HerSaturnReturns.com), interviewed queer women of color turning thirty, wrote *Saturnistas: The Play*, and broke up with my girlfriend to marry my best friend, determined to have a child with someone I could trust.

The book placed in my hands during the dinner party was *Conditions: Five / The Black Women's Issue. Conditions* became a common reading of mine. The spine would jump out at me at Lesbian Herstory Archives events, during lesbian-feminist house-sits, at dinner parties, or as the bookshelf banter of first dates. I learned that the text came at a time of both sparsity and new energy in lesbian publishing. By nature of its community-focused distribution and publication strategies, *Conditions* became a catalyst, or lifeline, or game changer for so many lesbians in their late twenties/early thirties (Saturn) experiences. I cannot resist but mention that when I was twenty-seven (in 2010), *Conditions: Five* would have been completing its Saturn Return at its thirty-one-year anniversary.

Yet, ten years after my intro to *Five*, I surveyed *Conditions: Two* for the first time for this special issue of *Sinister Wisdom*. It was easy for me to be reflective while reading. By its very existence it seems the community chose this journal to continue. The issue itself was about choice-making. The very nature of this being the second issue led my first response to *Two* to be subtle, suspending me in a kind of wistfulness. I was reminded of my Saturn choices as responses to tumult, but also for how they bound me to community, and the relationships I built. Each contribution sparked a memory from my Saturn journey.

The issue begins with Patricia Jones's "Mi Chinita Poem," which led me to recall my marriage. Jones's reference to her Cubana heritage within a foreign city landscape reminded me of my best friend and wife, Jaz, who is forever a Puerto Rican powerhouse riding the train from da Bronx. Jaz, whom I met when I was seventeen, was my rock for a solid ten years before I proposed. Jones begins her piece referencing the distances that being a part of a non-normative culture may lead to, that "the real american does not know what flan is" (7). I likely married Jaz because her cousin makes flan, and I knew that our daughter would know what flan is. She had it at three years old, and now she still calls it cheesecake and thinks that it is a side that comes with pizza takeout.

Susan Kronenberg's "Seriphos" reminds me in her first line that "I was the foreigner" (13). Her piece led me to the moments spent with my actual real-life Brooklyn friends, Alexis and Zahra, neither of whom ever met each other, but it was Kronenberg's 1975 acknowledgement of being someone "with no friends or relatives to see me off" (13), especially after I left Brooklyn to another state entirely, that I knew the friendships that I would take with me.

Barbara Smith's "Toward a Black Feminist Criticism" reminded me of the tumult caused by aiming to merge my personal life with my professional. Her inclination toward pointing out that "I do not know where to begin" (25) represented the feeling at the center of my overcompensation in modeling Black lesbians and "the pain of their absence" (26). Often, the answer was extreme: either hyper-formality or performance art. This duality of existence led me to Michelle, my doppelganger who became a close friend and lover (I actually don't think that we look alike—but who decides?). In reading Smith, I see now that Michelle and me were like Sula and Nel in that my denial of the kind of love we shared was akin to the denial of my undergrad Black women's literature professor who practically failed me for implying a lesbian relationship in Morrison's text. Michelle was my *girl, girl, girl* and it wasn't until she found love elsewhere that I realized the kind of love she was open to sharing with me. That silence between Michelle and I, the inability of me to articulate our truth, is what broke us. That silence is present in Smith's essay. It is this loud silence, the presence of absence, that I find in common with Black lesbians—an inability to remark on emotion that centers our *own* hearts, leaning instead to the politicos. Our relationship was "inherently lesbian" (39), yes, I see that now, but I would go further to say that it was inherently Black lesbian, despite it not being that at all.

Speaking of silences, Elly Bulkin's "An interview with Adrienne Rich Part II" begins with, "You keep getting back to the silence about loving women" (53). It took years of monthly meetings with my Black lesbian writing group of three, my two comrades Tara and Olivia and me, before I realized how deeply I loved them both. We recited each other's work out loud and embraced Rich's dream of a common language. "It was the power of the poem" (53) in Olivia's Brooklyn flat that brought me whole at her kitchen table, where we lavishly poured wine and smoked cigarettes past the curtain and instigated "the fact that there's no language to pull out, in some way" (56) that could ever describe a friendship like ours. Years later I would stand before Tara and Olivia's friends and family, my six-month-old in front-row in Jaz's arms, officiating them as partners for life. That night we danced and danced, and Olivia whispered in my ear, under the strength of the music, that she was finally pregnant.

At some point, I did end up leaving Brooklyn during my Saturn; I moved to the Bronx, which is still in NYC, but for us New Yorkers, it may as well have been across the Atlantic. I grew nostalgic for Brooklyn. Forgetting my brother's or cousin's murder from gun violence, instead I replayed moments of lesbian love. Melanie Kaye's "Amazons" resurrected the unending image of Brooklyn dykes as "they came astride grey horses dappled with sun" (67). One girlfriend of mine, Arianne, was quite Amazonian. Her love will forever be a gif on loop of an opening palm revealing the head of a stemless pink peony, pushing its center to my nose.

My post-Saturn choices led me to Connecticut, a commuter state that leans on New York City. And the reasons that brought me here are what had me anchored to Irena Klepfisz's "Women Without Children/Women Without Families/Women Alone." Isn't it true that at "the center of my bleakest fantasy is the shopping-bag lady" (72)? When recalling the many relationships that have curated my movements, there are those that, like Klepfisz, both paralyzed me and led me forward: my mother and my daughter— for their love and estrangement.

I should say that there is nothing glamorous about mothering. It was the ancestral pull that led me to want to be pregnant, but the child-raising is isolating, fear-filled, and relates to nothing I've ever known. The lesbian community, for all of its poetry and community-building and talk of love, does not prepare you for C-sections, nursing, and worse, the lifetime of detachment. There was nothing in lesbian-feminist writing that discussed the true trauma of weaning, the ripping away of a child, or that mothering is actually the measured art of slow separation—myself from community, and my daughter and me from each other.

Or, I should say, there was nothing alluding to this in my reading until now.

Georgette Cerrutti's "Between Mother and Me" made the case so clearly that "I have lost a lot of it but" (86) my mother has more loss than me. One of my earliest memories of my mom, "when I was twelve" (87), we rushed out of the car from my dad's Ethiopian Orthodox church, and instead of the usual "we're home" yell across the house, we walked in slowly. My dad, with his pointer finger to his lips, used his toes to enter silently, and we mimicked. From the back room came the sound of a voice singing a Diana Ross ballad, and there she was, back-flat on a bed, eyes closed, headphones, tape deck, feet tapping, arms pressuring the air, the most free I'd ever seen her, our giggles "not loud enough" (88). My dad finally approached, yelling, "Judy, you can sing!" My mom nearly fell off the bed. She stopped singing. We stopped laughing. "Even now I am afraid of a certain quiet" (88).

It is the fear of the shopping-bag lady—becoming despised and useless to society, someone "on a subway . . . oblivious to the other people in the car, while an invisible circle seems to form around her. No one will come near her, no one will sit close to her, no one will risk being touched by her" (73). That fictional image Klepfisz was able to capture was likely at the center of my Saturn tumult. The woman I dared not become was wrapped in the timeline of needing to do something before I was too old, and knowing that there could be no happy accidents. It all had to be planned—a donor sought, infertility coverage secured, ovulation tracked, papers signed. The choice to wed my best friend and conceive was the answer to my dreams, a flight away from the flames, and a call to the voice of a crying child who was waiting for me to birth her.

Now at thirty-nine my daughter is here, though the community has gone, replaced with mostly memories, and a feeling: akin to a kind of wistfulness.

Shawn(ta) Smith-Cruz co-edited the Lesbian Herstory Archives (LHA) and MichFest issues of *Sinister Wisdom*. She is a librarian, writer, mother, daughter, and granddaughter to Garifuna and Jamaican women. A volunteer co-coordinator at LHA, she is a recipient of the 2020 WGSS Award for Significant Achievement in Women's & Gender Studies in Librarianship from the Association of College and Research Libraries, and a 2020 nominee for the Pushcart Prize for "What the Trees Said" in *Sinister Wisdom* 118. Shawn teaches graduate library students at Pratt School of Information, is the Associate Dean for Teaching, Learning, and Engagement at NYU Division of Libraries, and wishes she had more time to write lesbian fiction and play hide-and-seek with her little post-Saturn miracle, Joey.

CONDITIONS: THREE
— Response by Sarah Schulman

The Struggle to Think for Ourselves: Reflections on Conditions: Three (1978)

There was an early twentieth-century experimental writers' journal called *The Introspectivist* that commented on the literary currents of the 1920s. These cutting-edge artists inserted themselves into the business of modernism but were never heard because the magazine, *In Zikh*, was in Yiddish. The price of keeping your own culture alive and evolving was separation. In many ways, feminist and lesbian artists repeated this conundrum—and forty years later, the marginalization continues. Hence, the long overdue retrospective view on the historic and foundational *Conditions* magazine takes place in *Sinister Wisdom*, under the guidance of its gifted visionary editor Julie Enszer, instead of in the *New Yorker* or the *New York Review of Books*.

This persistent disregard from American letters has nothing to do with quality and everything to do with currency. Point of view dictates exclusion more than story and more than the author's demographics. In the arts, reward and recognition have nothing to do with quality of achievement. Good work can be rewarded, but not because it's good; recognition is based most often on branding, relationships, and how much the apparatus can use an author's profile or achievement to elevate their own value.

Conditions: Three seems to have three purposes: 1) to meld straight and lesbian interracial work into a non-homophobic/anti-racist feminist vision; 2) to cohere and elevate the movement/community's social and aesthetic discourse so that it is legible; and 3) to review lesbian and feminist works appropriately when, for the most part, they are ignored by the mainstream.

Now, of course, we know the punchline. These goals evolved successfully for about fifteen years—surpassing the election of Ronald Reagan, the incremental chipping away at the gains of the previous era. Ultimately, marketing, branding, gentrification, and the usurpation and weakening of feminist tropes and lesbian images by corporate entertainment destroyed this work. When the underground was the only place to be reflected, it served as a fertile authority. When it became replaced by niche marketing, the queer consumer and what I called "fake public homosexuality" emerged (see *Stagestruck: Theater, AIDS, and the Marketing of Gay America* [1998]). The dynamic energy represented by *Conditions* dissipated into smaller, still underground, conversations.

It is evident from the table of contents of *Conditions: Three* that Jewish reckoning is a significant concern to the *Conditions* collective. A number of works, most notably by Francine Krasno, Enid Dame, and Rima Shore (in a funny, eccentric "Russian" play), are grounded in Eastern European connections; *Conditions: Three* was published thirty-three years after the end of the Holocaust. But lineage is a huge theme of this issue, surpassing any particular identity. Family, community, and legacy as foundations of contemporary consciousness are prominent in a number of works by women of color. Barbara Noda writes about her farmworker father; Alice Walker's short story connects a son's political consciousness to the narrator's father's grandmother's enslavement. Nellie Wong's ten-part poem is a cumulative counting of Asian women from mother to comrade, each relationship demanding a coming to grips. Roots, connections, ancestors, descendants—at this moment, extending the family tree horizontally without losing one's history is a labor of concern for *Conditions* writers.

Sandra Maria Esteves reminds us "Bedford Hills is a Women's Prison" by making that fact the title of her poem. The expositional quality, a sometimes overused "I" makes some of the poetic work dated, but Marilyn Hacker's quirky, brainiac language play in "Boulder: August 1977" is still mysterious:

Curves converge and blossom in your face;
leaf-shapes ripple a patterned snake
safe through pied grass. A tacky diamond back

Similarly, fiction in this issue also relies on the foregrounded first person. The essays are an entirely different ball game and the strength of the issue. The struggle to think for ourselves is visible in aesthetic and intellectual tensions.

"Homophobia and Romantic Love" by Jane Rule appears in *Conditions: Three*. While contemporary readers may know her for *Desert Hearts*, a lesbian cult-classic film and novel that seems to have fallen off the radar, Rule was a highly respected Canadian novelist who took a number of bold stands for sexual freedom and sexually explicit material. Her subject is the heartfelt and sincere struggle to create lesbian relationships independent from heterosexual models. This was very hard to imagine and to apply. As Adrienne Rich (whose influence is apparent throughout the volume) said, "compulsory heterosexuality" was the dominant pressure in every woman's life. In this essay, Rule asks, "Are we the unclean bitches who must transform ourselves into goddesses?"

The most interesting essay is by the iconoclastic Michelle Cliff, a Jamaican writer who works in assembled fragments that resonate and thereby reveal stories. Hers is a memory of childhood in a wealthy home: maids, poor people washing their clothes in her family's river, families who own sugar mills.

Reviews, literary conversations, comprise half the volume and clearly are its heart. Barbara Smith reviews three works by Pat Parker. "When I first read Parker's work" Smith writes, "I was much more excited by the content than by the execution of her verse." Smith goes on to reveal that only when she heard Parker read in person did she understand that this poetry was not intended solely for the page, but was instead strongly rooted in the Black oral tradition. Reading this review reminded me of a roundtable appearing in a later issue of *Conditions*, *Conditions: Nine*, that is seared in my memory. Cheryl Clarke, Jewelle Gomez, Evelynn Hammonds, Bonnie Johnson, and Linda Powell—all Black women writers—discussed aesthetics, and Pat Parker's work came up.[1] This same issue was raised with some writers pointing out the lack of subtext in Parker's work, the literal language. And as I recall, Clarke grappled with these criticisms, saying something to the effect that "anyone who inspires so many Black lesbians to become writers is a successful artist" (paraphrase from memory). In this way, Smith raises questions about aesthetics that are still alive and dynamic in many milieus and places in the culture.

Turning the pages reminds of many writers who deserve retrospectives. For example:

Irena Klepfisz, not only a writer but also a force in the creation of the Yiddish revival, and the rearticulation of a new Jewish politics of Israel/Palestine; Judy Grahn, an experimental writer working both literally in the telling of working-class stories, and with formal invention in a wide range of books on subjects as different as Gertrude Stein's poetics to tarot cards; and Meridel Le Sueur, whose "Worker Writers" is a classic text highly deserving of new attention.

Probably the most significant moment in *Conditions: Three* is the announcement in the back of an upcoming volume, *Conditions: Five / The Black Women's Issue*, co-edited by Barbara Smith and Lorraine Bethel—a publication that changed women's publishing. A precursor to Kitchen Table: Women of Color Press, it was to that date the most significant gathering of Black straight and gay women's voices in print.

The issue ends with ads for the disappeared: women's bookstores, women's magazines like *Heresies, off our backs, Black*

1

Editor's Note: The article referenced is "Black Women on Black Women Writers: Conversations and Questions in *Conditions: Nine* (1983), pages 88–137. The interlocutors are Cheryl Clarke, Jewelle Gomez, Evelynn Hammonds, Bonnie Johnson, and Linda Powell.

Maria, *Radical Teacher*'s special issue on women's studies, *Dyke Quarterly*. These are artifacts from a grossly unexplored history, unknown by new generations. If the history of the lesbian and feminist contribution will ever be accurately told, these pages will have to be harvested, taught, valued, and, most challengingly, understood on their own terms.

Sarah Schulman is a novelist, playwright, screenwriter, nonfiction writer, AIDS historian, journalist, and active participant citizen. Schulman is co-founder of MIX: NY LGBT Experimental Film and Video Festival, co-director ACT UP Oral History Project (www.actuporalhistory.org), and US coordinator of the first LGBT Delegation to Palestine. She is the author of ten novels, including *The Cosmopolitans* (2016), *The Mere Future* (2010), and *People in Trouble* (1990). She is the author of five nonfiction books, most recently *Let the Record Show: A Political History of ACT UP* (2021).

CONDITIONS: FOUR
— Response by Andrea Canaan

Saving Women's Voices and Lives

We work collectively to select and edit material which will reflect women's perceptions of themselves, each other, the conditions of their lives, and the world around them.

—*Conditions: Four*, statement of purpose

Conditions: Four was among a number of literary journals and magazines that printed the work of women writers I learned from, and, in significant part, saved my sanity and my life. In addition to *Conditions, Quest, HERESIES, the second wave, Women & Literature*, and *Sinister Wisdom* provided the poetry, fiction, and nonfiction songs of my authentic living. They provided myriad oases of feeling, thinking, and doing that countered the invisibility, the isolation, the enforced heterosexuality, the expected silence, and the expected self-denial that my family, my community, and the cultures at large required. This generation of women writers and publishers constructed intentional, conscious, and national creative community networks that would enable me to recognize, accept, and live with all of the parts of myself intact: Black, woman, Southern, radical, feminist, lesbian, and activist—on behalf of women and children and against racism, antisemitism, violence, homophobia, misogyny, xenophobia, and war.

I graduated from high school in New Orleans in 1968, the first year public schools were desegregated in Louisiana. My friends refused to disrupt our senior year by enduring the hate of white students and teachers at a previously all-white school. We refused to bow to pressure from the civil rights movement, our parents, and our community to be the *first* to integrate, to be part of the galaxy of *first* Black achievements at the cost of great personal suffering.

I came home after a walk with my girlfriends to the snowball stand a few blocks away. The stand was in the middle of the block at Granny Ethel's house. Granny Ethel made five fruit flavors, as well as vanilla ice cream, that could top the snowballs. Her granddaughters pulled the lever on the ice machine that shot out the snow-ice and took in the twenty-five cents for the largest cone. With our lips and shirts turning red, blue, orange, and green, we sat on Magnolia Project stone benches and enjoyed the cool breeze that announced a late afternoon shower. At the first clap of thunder, we scattered home. I found my favorite Sunday school teacher and the head of Mt. Zion United Methodist Church's usher board sipping coffee at our kitchen table. After respectful greetings and hugs, my mother said, "Miss Genevieve and Miss Val want to talk to you about going to Fortier this school year."

I groaned inside and disciplined myself not to roll my eyes and sigh out loud. I sat down and listened politely.

"Now we hear that you and your best church friends have decided not to integrate, and we wonder why that is?"

It wasn't a question.

"You should be proud to integrate Fortier High School. You're smart, sure to go to college, and you're strong," my mother said. "Do you understand how important this is for all of us?"

That was a question. My mother looked at me with the expectation that I should stay polite and answer correctly.

"Yes, ma'am," I said.

"Good girl," they said in unison. My mother smiled in approval.

They took "yes, ma'am" as acquiescence. They looked to my mother to continue to prepare me to integrate. My friends and I knew not to tell them how we felt or defy them directly. Instead, we applied the principles of passive resistance. Our mothers quietly folded beneath our silent refusal to integrate and helped us get ready to cheer for our football and basketball teams, our prom in our gym, our plays and operettas, our holiday dances, and our office workers, the teachers, cafeteria workers, and janitors celebrating us, showing us how proud of us they were. We knew we would forfeit all of that in the name of integration. We didn't want to become stoic stone features in the presence of the threatening glares of white parents, teachers, and students. On the first day of school in 1967, we went to our high school with all Black students, all Black teachers, and all Black administrators.

In college I participated in taking over university buildings. We protested the university's acceptance of extreme racist disparities between the segregated Louisiana University systems, LSU for whites and Southern University for blacks. Southern University received a fraction of the funding of LSU and paid professors much less. The buildings, libraries, labs, gym, athletic equipment, and facilities, and their upkeep, were fourth rate by comparison. In November of 1972, I witnessed my fellow protesting students being shot and killed. The deaths of white Kent State students earlier that year made national news. African American students shot and killed at Jackson State and Southern University received very little national attention. After college, I continued to march and raise consciousness, participating in the anti-war, anti-apartheid, anti–violence against women, lesbian, gay, and Black Power movements.

Many women's voices and lives were saved by queer entrepreneurs, bookstores and collectives, women publishers, small presses, journals, magazines, and newspapers that spoke to the vibrant, sexy, creative lives of bulldaggers, KyKy girls, closeted women, and lesbians. In this flourishing era, we saw our lives waiting for us on the page.

In 1979, I was a twenty-nine-year-old Southern African American mother of a four-year-old daughter. I *came out* in white feminist communities because there were no *out* Black lesbians in New Orleans in 1979. I fully embraced my identity as a radical—out—Black lesbian feminist anyway. Soon I understood why so many lesbians, Black and white, lived so fiercely in the closet. In 1980 I was fired from my job with the Louisiana State Bureau for Women for saying in a staff meeting that I was Black, lesbian, and feminist.

I sued the state of Louisiana on First Amendment grounds, with the ACLU representing my case. To raise money for the case, I traveled around the country with Kendal, a white lesbian writer, mother, and beloved friend. Kendal and I were supported by a network of independent women's bookstores and women's writing communities across the US. They befriended us, helped me raise money for my case, set up our readings, provided transportation, and housed and fed us.

In my suit against the State of Louisiana, I appeared in the Louisiana State Court and in the United States Court of Appeals for the Fifth Circuit. The only people who sat with me in court were members of my white lesbian community. My Black community was absent and silent. I had tried to come out to my mother. She shushed me, refused to hear when I began to speak about being in love with a woman and knowing I was lesbian. When I made the decision to sue the State of Louisiana, I spoke through my mother's defenses, came out to her, and explained why I was fired. I gathered the women matriarchs of my extended family, women who were beloved mothers to me. I came out to them. I told them that it was likely there would be newspaper coverage of the court proceedings. I called them all together to tell them what was about to happen because my mother and all of the matriarchs always admonished us.

"Don't you ever let anybody tell me anything about you that I don't already know."

My mother wept bitter tears. My elders were silent in the presence of my mother's anguish. My mother felt judged by her friends, neighbors, and church members. She knew they thought she had failed to raise me right, because maybe she wasn't right. She knew how they thought and felt, because it was what she had felt and thought and said of others. When I appeared very briefly on television coming down the steps of the United States Court of Appeals for the Fifth Circuit, I did affirm reports that I was indeed a radical Black lesbian feminist. My mother fled to the home of extended family and took to her bed for months.

I was evicted from my home twice. The State blocked my unemployment compensation. The Louisiana State Court ruled that Louisiana had, in fact, protected my First Amendment rights of free speech. On appeal, the Fifth Circuit Court disagreed. It found that my speech was, in fact, protected and the Louisiana Bureau for Women had, indeed, fired me based on my protected speech. The decision became precedent in Louisiana case law and on the Fifth Circuit. However, the court refused to reinstate me or pay me back wages. The Louisiana Bureau for Women argued they could have fired me for other causes. The causes presented were petty and thin, but they were enough for the court. With no job, no support from my family and Black community, I decided to leave my home. I moved to the Bay Area.

In 1979, I opened a copy of *Conditions: Four* that had passed through many hands before it reached mine. I read it in the way I still read literary magazines and journals. First, I read front matter, table of contents, classifieds, submissions, and announcements of coming issues, and then I read the issue from back to front and from front to back, savoring each creative and scholarly work like breath, like air, like milk and honey. I was astonished by the rush of memories of writers and activists who had been my teachers and mentors, along with writers I had studied with and had made creative, political, named family with. I had this same feeling when I found a box of my old journals when we moved recently. I was staggered by the generation of women's voices that had rested on the page waiting for me to read them again, for me to see, hear, and feel the writers, lesbian and straight, women of color and white, who had updated and refabricated feminist theory, literary criticism, and creative writing genres of nonfiction, fiction, journaling, poetry, and science fiction from the half-century past for the half-century coming.

Conditions: Four contributors, reviewers, and editors included teachers I would later study with: Jan Clausen, Irena Klepfisz, Michelle Cliff, and Audre Lorde. This same issue featured writers who would be my co-contributors to *This Bridge Called My Back: Writing by Radical Women of Color*, including Audre Lorde, Barbara Smith, Beverly Smith, and Nellie Wong. In the first years of coming out, I learned a great deal by reading the women's writing, such as Pat Parker's *Woman Slaughter*, Adrienne Rich's *Of Woman Born*, Octavia E. Butler's *Patternmaster*, Audre Lorde's *Black Unicorn*, Andrea Dworkin's *Woman Hating*, Alice Walker's *In Love and Trouble*, and Maya Angelou's *I Know Why the Caged Bird Sings*. From their writing, writing practices, public reading, teaching, and activism, I learned ways to build my own foundations as a writer that eventually led me to gift myself with a writer's life. My writer's life includes a daily writing practice, building and sustaining a writing community, and feminist-womanist activism.

Conditions: Four featured poetry by Judith McDaniel, Marilyn Krysl, Jeanne Finley, Nellie Wong, Robin Silberman, Diana Bellessi, and Lyn Lifshin; a prose poem by Michelle Cliff; fiction by Janet Sternburg, Erika Duncan, Susan Krieger, Ellen Garvey, and Sandy Boucher; essays by Audre Lorde, Barbara Smith and Beverly Smith, and Stephanie Golden; and reviews by Pamela Trunk, Jan Clausen, Rima Shore, Gloria T. Hull, Elly Bulkin, Blanche Wiesen Cook, and Liz Hess.

In Jan Clausen's review of Nelly Wong's *Dreams in Harrison Railroad Park*, a small book of poetry that reveals Wong's connection to her ancestors, her parents, her heritage, and herself, Clausen describes this small book of poetry as "providing a context for self-exploration, a basis for self-transformation" (129). Clausen examines the poems critically. She names the places where Wong's poems are reflective, mingle anger with humor, and excel at the story poem form:

Wong is a materialist in the best sense; her work is grounded in physical and economic realities. Hers is a woman's deeply ingrained consciousness of the everyday tasks that sustain a life, the details which renders it pleasant or unbearable. (132)

Blanche Wiesen Cook reviews *The Notebook That Emma Gave Me: The Autobiography of a Lesbian* by Kay Van Deurs. Wiesen Cook describes Deurs as a privileged, white Southern daughter of an admiral confronted with familial, social, and mental adversity as a nonconforming woman in the 1950s. Deurs emerges with a "searching, politically engaged and creative life." (152)

It is an unconventional book, neither fiction nor standard autobiography. Filled with a mixture of narrative passages, fragments of letters, and journal entries, it is charmingly written. (153)

A surprise in this review: Wiesen Cook critiques Deurs's ending of the book with an angry letter to Holly Near, a feminist, activist, songwriter, and performer. In the letter, Deurs characterizes Near as coming from a Marxist, left, male point of view. Wiesen Cook critiques the placement of the letter at the end of the book as giving it more weight than if it had been placed earlier. Wiesen Cook shares her different view of Marxism and feminism in a letter addressed to Deurs that ends her review of the book.

Marxism and feminism are indeed two separate things. And they do not AUTOMATICALLY go together. But socialism and feminism NEED each other, desperately and urgently. (154)

The *Conditions* reviews introduced me to books I would otherwise not have known existed and provided me with myriad portals to creative feminist thinking and living. As a Black woman and mother of a daughter, I was confronted in the '80s with issues of lesbians deciding to live their lives without the presence of men, including male children. I understood and agreed that women who decided to live in environments without maleness should live as they wished. I was committed to creating and preserving spaces for women and girls to gather and create in the powerful expressions of being female. I also reserved the same for being among Black women and girls. I continued to be committed to my relationships with boys and men.

I attended the Michigan Womyn's Music Festival in the '70s. It was a wonderland of women and women's music. I didn't take my daughter because I had excellent childcare. When the festival placed restrictions on mothers of boy children, I stopped going to the festival. I knew I would not be separated from my daughter because she was female. I also knew mothers of boy children faced being separated from their children while attending the festival. I refused to exercise the privilege afforded to me as the mother of a girl child while mothers of male children, and the boy children themselves, were cruelly discriminated against and disempowered.

In this issue of *Conditions: Four*, an essay appears by Audre Lorde about raising a Black male child, "Man Child: A Black Lesbian Feminist Response." In this essay Audre begins:

This article is not a theoretical discussion of Lesbian Mothers and their sons. Nor is it a how-to article. It is my attempt to scrutinize and to share some pieces of that common history belonging to my son and me. (30)

She continues:

Raising black children female and male in the mouth of a racist, sexist, suicidal dragon is perilous and always chancy. . . .
    I wish to raise a black man who will not be destroyed by, nor settle for, those corruptions that are called power by the

white fathers who mean his destruction in the same ways that they mean mine. I wish to raise a black man who will recognize that the legitimate objects of his hostilities are not women, but the system which programs him to fear and despise women as well as his own black self. (31)

Audre Lorde's essay affirms and teaches me how to commit to being a safe and loving adult in the lives of female and male children, how to support their mothers, and how I would insist on being supported as a parent.

Barbara and Beverly Smith's essay, "I Am Not Meant to Be Alone and Without You Who Understand: Letters from Black Feminists, 1972–1978," reflects my experience and reality at that time:

There are several recurring themes which run through the letters: our isolation from other Black feminists and within the women's movement; the painful realities of white women's racism in the movement; commentary on heterosexuality and marriage; coming out as Lesbians; homophobia in the Black community; and our involvement with Black women's culture. (63)

I am forever grateful for the writers, reviewers, advertisers, and editors of *Conditions* and publications like it. In significant part, it was because of these publications that I did find a sustaining Black lesbian community in the Bay Area. Many lesbians and feminists rejected norms of femininity. Some of my newfound sisters wore Birkenstocks, flannel shirts, didn't wear bras, didn't shave legs or underarms, didn't wear makeup, and didn't have relationships with straight women. Some in my Black and white lesbian-feminist communities sought to have me conform to one or more sets of lesbian-specific expectations. While I did wear Birkenstocks, I never shaved anyway, and bras had always been optional for me.

I didn't own a flannel shirt, and I kept and made close relationships with the straight women in my family and old friends. I made new ones and I wore lipstick.

Andrea Canaan, MSW, MFA, retired clinical social worker and social service administrator, is a mother, activist, memoirist, and novelist. She was a contributor to *This Bridge Called My Back: Writings by Radical Women of Color*. Canaan sued in *Canaan v. the State of Louisiana* on free speech grounds when she was fired for saying she was a Black lesbian-feminist. In the process of publishing a memoir, *Black Magnolia*, and a novel, *A Thousand Crowning Sorrows*, Andrea is the founder of A Writer's Life writing and wellness coaching that includes individual and group writing and wellness practices. She currently lives in Rio Vista, California.

CONDITIONS: FIVE / THE BLACK WOMEN'S ISSUE

— Response by Mecca Jamilah Sullivan

The Club[1]

Our Third World lesbian spaces will come
from those of us who are remembering in increasing
numbers

---

1 A fast and loose riff on *Conditions: Five / The Black Women's Issue* (1979), revisiting the style of Alice Walker's "Coming Apart," published in *Take Back the Night: Women on Pornography* (William Morrow and Company, 1980), edited by Laura Lederer). For contemporary readers, *Conditions: Five* offers a stunning gathering of black feminist voices. At the time of its publication, it caused significant controversy for its refusal to silence black lesbian voices or subjugate black feminist sexuality. This criticism, linked to the "sex wars" of the early 1980s, reflects a politics of respectability and sexual silencing that persists in some areas of feminist discourse in 2020, particularly in the policing of black women's sexual self-expression. Where and how do black queer sex, sex workers, trans and nonbinary experience, and other disallowed realms of black gender and sexual being find safety and freedom in black feminist visions of futurity? This is a crucial question of our time. *Conditions: Five* lights a path for answering these questions, and reminds us that we've been here before. Edited by Barbara Smith and Lorraine Bethel, and containing works by Pat Parker, Gloria T. Hull, Audre Lorde, Beverly Smith, Demita Frazier, Cheryl Clarke, Alexis De Veaux, Donna K. Rushin, Ann Allen Shockley, and many others, *Conditions: Five* is a gathering space for the fullness, queerness, and complexity of black feminist being. In "The Club," I imagine such a figurative space in a not-so-distant physical future, considering how these writers, their characters, and the voices they conjure might inflect our own discussions about black feminist pleasure, safety, and freedom. I take up a speculative expository fiction approach, revisiting Walker's "Coming Apart," in which she uses allegorical fiction to contextualize and amplify feminist critiques of pornography collected in another important text of the era—the 1980 anthology *Take Back the Night*. It is in this story (itself a critique of porn) that Walker first introduces the term "womanism." Here, I tilt the allegory toward a sex-inclusive and pleasure-emphatic vision of *BlackQueerFeminism*, exploring spaces of subversive sexuality, bodily pleasure, and erotic labor and performance as sites of black feminist possibility not unlike the space that lies between the covers of *Conditions: Five / The Black Women's Issue*.

that imitation versions don't make it ...
Black lesbian writers
Third World women artists from all over
Meeting, joining forces, sharing sista energy
speaking to our own experiences and sensibility
without having to explain anything to each other
because we are each other's lives and words
— Lorraine Bethel, "What Chou Mean *We*, White Girl? Or,
the Cullud Lesbian Feminist Declaration of Independence"
(*Conditions: Five*, 90–91)

Five ran her tongue over her lipstick under her mask and pushed through the door, trying not to think of Angelina. It was August, humid, and the outside air clung to her skin even as the AC from the club smacked toward her. She was two hours early, but still she felt a deep relief on arriving. Today, she couldn't get to work soon enough. Clearly she wasn't the only one who felt that way—several dancers were there already, laying out their outfits, eating, talking shit, making out.

Renita, Will, Beverly, and Clemmon stood before the full-length mirror stretching, admiring their lines and curves as the formally trained dancers did. They swore they were true artists. And they were. Five had observed this with some bitterness when she first got to the club years ago, bracing herself for the kind of tired high-art/low-art battle that had played itself out ad nauseam in her own dance school experience, one of the reasons she'd quit. Sometimes that fight did surface backstage at the club, but to Five's surprise, when it did, it was quickly cut short in a brilliant turn of phrase, often from Renita, who would swivel her head in the midst of a tabletop pose and say, "We're all artists, y'all. Show me a living black woman who ain't." To this, Will and Clemmon murmured clear but indefinite affirmation, saying "You right, you right," agreeing, but giving themselves space to think on it some more.

As she pushed into the club, Five washed her hands, dropped her bags in the spray space, and gave a deep, maskless exhale as the Sani-Mist covered her. She waved at the bartender, Alex D, the nonbinary mixologist who had deep skin and a nameless sexy, and who made the best old fashioned you've ever had. Once, when Five asked what the secret to their old fashioned was, Alex looked at her matter-of-factly. "I put the Afrofuture in it," they said, then walked away with a twerk in their step.

Today, Alex D stood propped behind the bar talking with E.J., another dancer, about one of the club's favorite topics of discussion: black women and self-care. For Five, the phrase "self-care" rang hollow outside the club—it had been beaten to death since the start of the pandemic back in 2020, and now it seemed to mean everything from proper re-vaccination cycling to outlandish e-vacation splurges, to the latest pumpkin spice trend on white-girl Instagram. But at the club, the conversations enlivened her. So much of what happened here was self-care, truly, though Five wouldn't have phrased it that way. She would simply call it survival. The dressing, the talking, the rituals of hair and makeup, the cleaning, the protecting. The sex and the food. Even the dancing—the work itself—felt nourishing more often than not. The club was the first place Five had ever really felt that way, including everyplace she'd called home and every crew she'd called family. This, more than anything, was what kept her coming back to the club. And it was the reason she was here, at work, two hours early today.

She had not found the words to explain to Angelina that dancing at the club was her survival. It wasn't that Angelina disapproved of her work—not exactly. Angelina was older, but she was quiet and reserved in a way that made Five want to both protect her and tempt her at once. Five could sense that Angelina admired the freedom and heat of the club, but that she always felt herself an outsider. Angelina had grown up in a strict family steeped in old money and proper Black Middle-Class values, among which

143 ♀ Winter 2022

quietude, rigidity, and respectability were chief. To her credit, Angelina worked hard to free herself of these restraints—Five knew this was part of what drew them together. She liked watching Angelina surprise herself with her desire. She enjoyed luring her further and further into daring, seeing her pleased and startled by the sound of her own voice.

Five was also grateful to Angelina. It was thanks to her that they had a home—a cute two-bedroom with excellent public Wi-Fi in a state with no police and a relatively efficient Community Safety Bureau, one of the first to go firearm-free. They shared the apartment with Angelina's cats, Rachel and Rosalie, who didn't quite love Five but tolerated her well enough. Angelina was a teacher, and she spent her days in their brightly lit office Screen-Timing with her tenth- and eleventh-grade literature students in front of the room's vast bookshelves. Of all the things Angelina had brought into Five's life, her library may have been the best. Angelina's shelves were amply curated and meticulously arranged, with prose and poetry monographs from Arroyo Pizarro to *Zami*, and all the most important anthologies and journals: *Take Back the Night*, *The Black Woman*, *This Bridge Called My Back*, *Words of Fire*, *Mouths of Rain*, *Home Girls*, *Sinister Wisdom*, every issue of *Conditions*. Angelina had even installed a Home Assistant audio plug-in, multi-programmed from title to author to genre and back. Sometimes, between Angelina's Screen-Time classes, Five wandered into the office before work to stare at the colorful spines and pick the poet who would accompany her through her day. "Homie, show me *Living as a Lesbian*," she'd say. Within seconds, the room would bluster up in response: "*Living as a Lesbian*. Cheryl Clarke. Shelf Four. Row C. Enjoy, girl."

Five loved how Angelina had her shit together, how she could be counted on to know what the safe bet was and to make it every time. Five also loved playing the role of the young and irascible temptress. The thick-hipped dancer who encouraged Angelina to come out to her family, who held her hand while she let her body speak in bed. Still, even after Angelina had crept out the closet into the relative safety of their shared life, her daring would only go so far. Her vision of a black lesbian future was a home and marriage, gourmet cat food for Rachel and Rosalie, legality, normalcy, children.

"You know white picket fences are not viral insulators," Five had joked once. "They don't even make them anymore." Angelina smiled, flushed. "Whatever," she said. "Just give me my 2.5 kids, like they used to say, and we'll be good. Population law be damned."

Five wasn't opposed to this life intellectually, though having children would mean she would have to stay home from the club while Angelina taught, at least for a while, which she was not willing to do. Where Angelina craved the safe cocoon of acceptance, for Five, inconspicuousness was death. Five wanted freedom, self-possession, shamelessness. She wanted the warmth of her own spotlight and phenomenal sex. Angelina insisted their desires were not incompatible, but Five was not so sure. This was the cause of many fights between them. *Disagreements*, Angelina would call them, but still.

These were the *disagreements* that had pushed her from the apartment to the club two hours early today. Angelina had purchased three vials of sperm without telling her, and had made a down payment on a pair of identical wedding rings. "Not for now," she had insisted this morning when Five found out by reading the bank statement for their shared account. "Just for safekeeping. For the future!" But the presumption that this future should be neat and orderly and entirely of Angelina's devising—the expectation that Five should mute her pleasure for that vision—it made her skin hot. It made her need to move, to leave. She wasn't sure how far, or for how long. She breathed out again as she thought of it, trying to shake the conversation off her skin as she moved deeper into the club.

"You getting my cocktail ready, right?" She said to Alex D on the way to the dressing room. They stood striking, gorgeous, with teal eyeshadow and a bright blue bowtie. "My regular, please," Five continued. "Old fashioned. But make it next-level strong. It's already been one of those days."

"I got you, Five." Alex D smiled. "But is it the regular or is it next-level? There's a difference, you know. You gonna have to choose. She does know that right, Tsaba?" Tsaba was a yellow-skinned dancer with a pitchfork-shaped scar on her hand. She had volunteered for the first vaccine trials in 2021 and had the sight ever since. Tsaba looked at Five's forehead, then back at Alex, and rolled her eyes. "Yeah, she know."

"Fine," Five said, sighing through a smile. "Give me next-level then. That's what I need. I'll come get it before I dance."

The customers wouldn't arrive for another hour, but the house DJ, Flowers, had already started playing. Five loved the club's soundtrack—it was all blackgirl body and blackqueer raunch, a mix of classical tracks by Salt-N-Pepa, Queen Latifah, and MC Lyte, blended with golden age bangers by Foxy Brown, Lil' Kim, and Missy, and throwbacks by City Girls, Nitty Scott, Meg Thee Stallion, and Cardi B. Just now Flowers played an old-school Big Freedia song that made Five's muscles want to leap and her ass swing into motion.

She made her way to the dressing room, where Linda, Shari, and Ewar were talking in a close circle, vibing on the political potentials of black queer art from under a cloud of smoke. This was another pleasure of the club—close talking and touch. Outside, no one had seen hugs beyond family since the Before Times. But everyone who entered the club—dancer, customer, babymutha, whoever—was tested twice using the H. Lacks Instant-Test, which the club purchased monthly with money crowdfunded by the Taylor-McDade Dirty Computer IT Collective and the Muholi Arts Trust. This meant the club was safer than any other place in the country.

Five watched as the dancers talked, brushing shoulders, caressing skin without worry, a collage of lip gloss and neckties and leather and sequined bras. She basked in the dancers' flirtation, their loudness, the way they made their opinions known and refused to behave. This was what she wanted. What Angelina couldn't seem to see. The club was a wonderland of black bodies, genders, and voices, so that even on days when Five didn't feel like working, the space filled her with something she needed to get through the rest of her life. When she walked in the door, the mask came off and her body was misted and she felt herself yawn open, ready for what the night had to offer.

Unlike her life with Angelina, conversations at the club were different every day. The discussions about art were her favorite. The chance to sit and listen to these queer conversations about black creative force was like water to her. It was exactly what she'd been missing in school, and at home as a child, and in all the other spaces she'd been.

Sometimes, between sets, she and the other dancers sat and talked with the regulars, especially Michelle, the college student activist who looked at you like she was studying for a test and got all the dancers in their feelings about prison abolition. Sometimes Michelle brought her friends, Janet, Muri, Jones, and Rushin. And they sat backstage with the dancers eating Alex D's famous lemon-pepper wings and talking shit about trifling men or plotting revolution.

Then there was Pat, the beautiful brown-skin trickster with the gleaming eyes who stood at the doorway. With her fly jackets and mercilessly polished shoes, she made the dancers feel safer and clear of their direction just by standing there, reminding people where they were, helping them figure out where they needed to be. No one knew what Pat's exact title was—Five thought of her as part security, part creative director. She had a V-Port Immunity Passport Verificationist License, a formality for the club, but Pat wasn't one for titles. When white people or cishet men wandered to the doorway, slurring their speech and fumbling over her pronouns, she looked at them like their faces were punchlines and said, "Leave me to me and let's talk about you. Do *you* need directions home?"

This was how it was at the club. Every night was a study on how to do black queer life. Some called it Black feminism and some said that wasn't for them—that the phrase was old, something that went out with maskless hugs and live arena concerts years ago. Five was clear that all her feminism would need to be black and queer. And that's what it was for her: BlackQueer Feminism. But to her, it didn't matter so much what you called it—she knew it when she saw it: black people unbraiding gender and celebrating the strange in themselves, plotting against their pain and spinning pleasure into art, loving and fucking, wet and ready to re-weave the world.

In the spirit of this vision, Five connected with as many dancers as she could and made a point to learn their names and stories. It was a good way to keep from thinking about her fight with Angelina. There were so many dancers who came through the space, fat and thick and short and thin, those with immigration papers and those without, speaking all kinds of languages and serving all the queer genders you could think of. There was Jonetta, who had one arm and a hurricane of silver hair and could climb a pole faster than anyone. There was Chirlane, the quiet newbie from New York whose eyes brimmed with feeling, and Toi and Allegra, both proudly unchilded, who danced like their bodies were no one's but their own. There was a black girl named Becky, who moved like a windmill and always wore a rose in her hair. There were the songsters, Patricia, Hillary, Calla, and Mary; if you listened closely, you could hear them singing riffs and runs in shocking harmony with the music while they danced. Then there was Audre, the fat, black, half-blind ambidextrous aerialist. She was a powerhouse whose inversions shifted gravity. She made you think the ground was the air, and when she was flying, you were flying with her. There were rumors Audre owned the place, but she never commented either way.

This was another of the club's mysteries. More than once, it crossed Five's mind that someone should write a history of the club—a documentary, maybe, or a biopic, like the one Bambara's Revolution Black Film Collective made about the Combahee River Collective back in 2023. The club had so many origin stories they were hard to gather into a single thread. It had moved around, changed purposes and locations often over time and tellings. Some said it began as a weekly voting-rights fish fry hosted by Atlanta's most notorious 1960s bulldagger. Others said it started as a women-only speakeasy in Harlem during prohibition. Occasionally, Five overheard the college professor regulars, Barbara, Ann, and Gloria, talking about the history, their voices lifting up to bold tones in vibrant debate. They talked about the club with passion, as though it meant as much in their hearts and bodies as it did in their minds. And so they were part of the club, to Five and everyone else, though they would probably never get on stage and dance. Then again, scholars could surprise you. Five relished dancing for them, bumping extra low, grinding extra juicy before them while she listened.

One thing the scholars did agree on was that the club had no owner. It borrowed space, stayed around for a while, expanded, changed a little. Eventually, it attracted too much of the wrong kind of attention, and you would find even the off nights overrun with white people and cishets, winding in awkward mimicry of the dancers as though crashing a gay club for a bachelorette, their presence so space-taking it threatened to strip the walls of color. Then it was time to switch up, morph a little, and move on, cropping up new, different, and unexpected somewhere else.

In this way, Five thought, Angelina was not so unlike the dancers. She was predictable in some ways—her need for sameness and safety, her yearning to be right. But she had a way of popping up in a space and a form you wouldn't anticipate, a penchant for pleasant surprise. She had this in common with Five, too. Perhaps this was what frustrated Five most. If she'd felt that Angelina didn't understand her, it would have been easier. But Angelina did understand—knew her almost like she knew herself—and she judged her anyway. This was what hurt.

Five was lotioning up backstage when she heard Pat announce that Angelina was at the door. She appeared at the entrance looking hot and upset. Her plain pink mask covered her face, and her breath steamed against her spindly glasses. Pat screened her and checked her V-Port. "Sorry Ange," she said. "I have to."

Angelina nodded and finally Pat ushered her in. Five waited for her to unmask and spray so they could kiss, but Angelina lingered in the doorway, her mouth still covered. She looked around the space as though she'd never been there before. Patricia and Chirlane walked by with feathers in their hair.

"You can take your mask off, girl," Chirlane said, laughing. "We all safe in here."

Five watched as Angelina stepped under the spray mister, her mask still on. Five loved to watch the dancers spray-mist when they entered, their shoulders relaxing in a deep exhale as they washed off the rigid distance outside and opened to the closeness of the club. But Angelina remained stiff, uneasy.

"I just came to support, see what y'all are up to." Angelina said. "Screen-Time's down again so I had to cancel class." She looked away.

It was thirty minutes until opening, and the music began to play. The first-shift dancers began stretching, making last-minute repairs to their costumes, practicing spins and splits against the poles. Angelina looked back at Five. "I'm sorry about this morning. I'm just tired. Work and all."

"Yeah," Five said. This was their rhythm. Half-throated fights that never came to full volume, too-quick apologies that never reached full depth. Five was about to offer her own apology—she wasn't yet sure for what—when Afrekete walked by. "Scuse me, y'all," she said, managing to look them both in the eye at once. Afrekete was unanimously considered the club's most beautiful dancer. Part sky creature, part Sahara cat, with slow-blooming eyes and an easy smile, she looked at you in a way that pierced you, made you think she knew you. But then, always, she dropped your gaze quickly, as though she'd never seen you at all. Rumor had it she'd broken Audre's heart back in the day, but no one could confirm this. Now she sashayed past Five and Angelina, all hip and swinging thigh, her costume an elaborate puff of fruit cutouts and peach-colored tulle. She smiled, the melony smell of her lotion settling between them. She was stunning, surprising. Five felt both herself and Angelina lose their breath.

"I'm sorry," Angelina said again, this time with a tight laugh. She gestured to the corner, where Mocque, the club's accountant and trans-inclusion consultant, was practicing her pussy-pop handstands against the back wall in a leather bustier. "You can't tell me this is where you want to spend your life. This is the work you want to do?"

Five watched as Afrekete walked to the mirror beside Janet, bent into a forward fold, and shimmied herself up, her costume flapping over her bare behind. She did this a few more times, gave a pigeon-toed twerk. Then she ran over to the table where Pat and Audre were sitting and swiped a lemon-pepper wing, laughing.

"Look. I admire it. I really do," Angelina's voice went plaintive, siren-like. "I love your body. I love all our bodies. I love how we move. And I want us to love our bodies too. But I just wonder . . . why the stage and the lights? Why does it all have to be so big, so public? So loud? I mean, isn't there something to be said for privacy? Safety? As feminists, black queer folx, lesbians, whoever, don't we deserve that too? I mean, if we want it?"

"I don't want it," Five said. Now it was her turn to be surprised by her own voice. "If safety is the limit of your vision, I don't want it. What I want is BlackQueer Feminism. I want something queer and complex and contradictory, like us. Something that's as strange

and shameless and as much about our pleasure as we need to be. I
don't want anything else or anything less."

Customers had started to gather, some taking notes, others
just being nosy. The music got louder.

"Okay," Angelina said. She raised her voice, looking afraid. "I
hear you. I'm not shaming or whatever. I'm not. Sex and desire and
ass-shaking. It's all a part of it. I get it. It's just . . ." She hunched
her shoulders and gestured around at the dancers, laughing,
stretching, arranging their outfits and talking shit. Teasing each
other, kissing each other, breathing. "These women are so brilliant.
All these folx," she said. "Wouldn't we all be better off with y'all at
the library? Or making policy? Or even out in the street, protesting?
Someplace where real work can actually happen?"

Now the dancers began to gather: Gloria, Barbara, Beverly,
Cheryl, Becky, Audre, Lorraine, Donna, Ann, Toi, Pat. They stood
there, a dazzle of black skin and body, waiting. Five couldn't pull
her eyes off them.

"We are the library," she said, clear as night. "This is the school
and the Smithsonian. Show me a black queer woman surviving
that ain't an artist. Show me a black queer person living in
pleasure that don't deserve a Nobel prize."

The dancers watched Angelina watch them, all their states of
costume and undress. Five watched, too, wondering what she
would do if Angelina started to cry. They stood there, everything
quiet but the song playing from the speakers, a wail of black girl
raunch and wanting.

"Ok," Angelina said.

"You can take your mask off, baby," Alex D called from behind
the bar. "We all safe in here. Safe as we can be. Come on in. Let
yourself breathe."

"Ok," she said again. But she didn't move.

Five walked toward her slowly, her arm extended to help, but
Angelina pulled away. She stepped under the mister again and
Pat pushed the button, the air moistening and fog frosting the

plexiglass shield as Angelina pulled the cloth from her own face. She moved toward the dancers again, still clothed, but now, somehow, more naked than anyone.

The baseline thumped. Pat called the welcome greeting and the regulars flocked to their favorite seats as the first-shift dancers took the stage, a pageant of flags and leans and attitudes from floor to pole. The air smelled like lotion, and bodies, and sex, and good food. Irresistible. Five picked up the drink that was waiting for her at the end of the bar. Next-level. She handed it to Angelina, and they walked into the music.

Mecca Jamilah Sullivan, PhD, is the author of the short story collection *Blue Talk and Love* and winner of the 2018 Judith Markowitz Award for LGBTQ Writers. Her stories and essays have appeared or are forthcoming in *Best New Writing*, *The Kenyon Review*, *Callaloo*, *Feminist Studies*, *American Fiction*, *Prairie Schooner*, *Crab Orchard Review*, *TriQuarterly*, *GLQ: Lesbian and Gay Studies Quarterly*, *American Literary History*, *The Scholar and Feminist*, *American Quarterly*, *Public Books*, *Ebony.com*, *TheRoot. com*, *BET.com*, and others. She has earned support and honors from the Bread Loaf Writers Conference, Yaddo, Hedgebrook, Lambda Literary, the Publishing Triangle, the Mellon Foundation, the Center for Fiction, and the National Endowment for the Arts. Her forthcoming academic book, *The Poetics of Difference: Queer Feminist Forms in the African Diaspora*, explores the politics of poetic experimentation in global black women's art, literature, and hip-hop. She is Assistant Professor of English at Bryn Mawr College, and is completing a novel.

ANNOUNCING CONDITIONS: FIVE THE BLACK WOMEN'S ISSUE

Guest edited
by

Lorraine Bethel

and

Barbara Smith

"De nigger woman is de mule uh de world so fur as Ah can see."
—Zora Neale Hurston, *Their Eyes Were Watching God*, 1937

"You ask about 'preoccupations'. I am preoccupied with the spiritual survival, the survival *whole* of my people. But beyond that, I am committed to exploring the oppressions, the insanities, the loyalties, and the triumphs of black women. . . . For me, black women are the most fascinating creations in the world."
—Alice Walker, in *Interviews With Black Writers*, 1973

"If I could just tell you what it's really like

CONDITIONS: SIX

— Response by Cheryl Renee Hopson

Eleven Poems

my lover is a woman

eight years my senior
and like you
i feel good,
feel safe

and, hear me on this, patricia
my lover is also my wife—
i never would have believed it,
that i could be so bold—
"come see us, but don't
bring your" true self—
imbibed; and etched
into my girl self,
and by whom?
"never feel my father"
neglect me, and
"never hear my mother" say,
it's not what i'd want for you.

Images, Summer 2020

I watch you ride away in your blue jersey
I see the way your eyes open as if seeing a new bike
The white rush of a waterfall becomes a memory to put away,
                                                    and store
Your smile is like an open window and a breeze, welcoming

Foxy stranger, I love that you are 73

Your eyes become poems on the page
You move like the ocean, wild and surprising
Your smile is the orange haze of the sun setting along the
                                                    Chesapeake Bay
Your eyes become six years of making love

You are my favorite, a Bomb Pop, sweet and satisfying
You are a love song remixed and on repeat
You are a whisper in my ear at a Johnny Gill concert
You are sex on a ladder with a machete

You are power in the guise of a butch lesbian
You are the kindling to every banked fire
You are the stuff of my dreams and we're awake
You are thunder and I am the shaken one.

You are Sunday service music and the benediction
You are fresh-out-of-the-oven biscuits with honey butter
You are the first "Oh, God!" of my womanhood.
You are my body's way of getting my attention.

"You Remind Me of a Girl that I Once Knew"

Title after Usher Raymond

Meshell,
it was my sister
who introduced
me to you
and
who didn't say a word
but played
your song, and still
it wasn't until
this woman my age
and white, and
brunette, with short
hair, butch
sexy, perfect
skin, eyes beautiful
and smiling and
something more, looked
at me. And, well,
how much running
can one do
after   that?

"Lord, what kind of child is this?"

Title after Pat Parker

All that fear.
What was it for?

Where did it come from?
And the shame?

And the shame?

Clandestine viewings of *Kissing Jessica
Stein* in your own apartment, lights
lowered, and you hunkered down
on the sofa, frightened of being
caught, at what? And what else
could it have been at thirty-
one years old?

The Lesbian Sex Book
filled in the gaps between
two generations, at least, of
Black woman family disgust at
bulldaggers, a new word your
grandmother spat into your girlhood
as if disabusing herself of a
murderous,
evil
thing.

For the Record—

I learn, in part, from
watching Black women love
and jettison
love

Tracy singing,
"Baby, I got your number,"
and Alice dodging phone
calls?

I listen
and want to pack up
my wife, and our life, and move us
closer to where that used-to-be-good-
loving came into being: Alice of
the pristine complexion and cheeky
smile; Tracy's almost baritone
voice speaking love, and altogether
different with a bass guitar.

Legacy. Herstory, as
you've got to let the people know,
   1. You are here.
   2. You have been here.
   3. You anticipate continuing.
   4. For posterity.

Virginia Beach Bound, Circa 1985

he turns toward
her Mama, moves his
"Who *the fuck* are you?"
storm of a face close
to hers and drills
down with "Bitch,"
and "Stupid whore,"
and "Worthless,"
and her smart,
pretty, "yellow"
Mama, her big talking
with her sisters Mama,
"mean as a snake" when
she wants to be Mama,
known for
fighting back,
they say,

apologizes,

and

cries

And
being her mother's
daughter for ten years
she waits for her Mama
to "Bop him upside the head,"
and she waits. And
then she turns her girl

self, her big sister self
towards the baby girl,
and covers her ears,

Astonished.

Conditions: Six, 1980—

A thinking woman sleeps with dragons.
—Adrienne Rich

Not to try to speak for, but
to listen
to stand
in the gap, to
be a sounding board,
an ear
fine-tuned to
women and
the conditions of
their lives, which is to say
how they love, how
they find
freedom, how they
love

Of how the straight ones
with caché seemed
hell-bent on vilifying
and fictionalizing
as insane the women who did not crave
or seek out
"the zipless fuck," or
the unwashed penis of a stranger,
and instead who rhapsodized about a woman
with a smile like the first yellow
of spring in Kentucky,
circa 1973, about a woman
plump and sweet like a summer blackberry
on the tongue—

I read forty years
later, and listen for
what the women
tell me, the upfront
ones who said
I "drank until shitfaced for
twenty years, and marched in the second
Pride Parade," circa 1976,
and, I "waited on my lover, and wrote a poem
for my daughter upon the death of
her father," and, I "am a revolutionary
who became a mother
and left my child, a girl," and, I "got hooked
on heroin and brought the baby girl
along, and called it loved, but
looking back, I'm not so sure," and, I "wailed
as the gavel sounded, knowing summer would never
be enough, knowing I would never be enough," and
"My brother did not dance but beat me
until I ran."

When a Daughter Speaks—

You are the kind of woman
who can leave a
child behind, a
Daughter, and then
write about
The leave-taking, the
Whys and
not the hows—

to drop a word like "revolutionary"
[a cage against mothering]
as if to explain,
to lament the years
lost? To you?

To me?

In my mother's story
I am loved, and
A distraction?

Daughter,
This is what it means
To be born to a woman
Revolutionary
To be said goodbye to
To force sacrifice from your
Heart, to be convinced of
Your mother's love.

Daughter,
This is what it means
To know your mother.

"But defiance is as eminent as change"

Title after Cheryl Clarke

Listen, Mother,

I have long forgotten
Your voice, and think of
Your giving birth to me as
A momentary cessation of
Movement from your running
Of underground missions of saving
Girls like me or like I was from
the kind of people you left me among,
Knowing as you must that family
Does not mean safe distances from
Boogey men and monsters;
And with no one there to lullaby me, and
no one's tired voice saying "Sleep,
child. I'll be here when you awake."

Even if the child is a daughter.

Mother, this love is a child's love,
all needing
and wanting to be seen.

Equality

Every second of every
Minute of every day
Of every year of
Every decade, of every century,
A signal, something
To suggest an end to
This
Unnecessary living on our
Knees as if
Genuflecting to this
Cosmic
Thing
Meant to bring a woman down
Meant to suffocate
Meant to put an end to
To blot out
To spirit away with
The truth that
Everything pleasurable
That warms
From the center
That is inextinguishable
That is desire

Is born of a woman.

This Is Just to Say—

For R.D.

The night I saw you
I knew you knew I was there.
Call it arrogance. Call it
delusion. Call it
what it is—an electric
current that zips lines
between two people,
and
at this age I
do not think anything
more than love is,
and lust and, so, I noted
the slowing down
of my breathing,
and the rising heat at
my neck, and smiled
at my body's reminder
that a pretty, natural-
haired, deep
brown, muscled, thin waist,
nice
booty, yoga aficionado,
motorcycle driving,
make me wanna holla,
"good, gawd," take a sip
of my cocktail *fine*
Black woman loving
woman, is in my midst.
Anyway, this is just to say,
I was thinking about you.

Artist Statement

I am a poet, professor, essayist, and scholar. I am as well the lone survivor of three biological sisters, all smart, funny, charismatic, and imperfect pretty-faced Black women, two of whom were mothers. My oldest sister's last communication to me was 1) "I love you just the way you are," check, and 2) "Write our story." Older sisters are notoriously bossy, and mine was no exception. Still, I love and embrace my big sister's charge. The poems contained herein are dedicated to my sisters, to Doris Lunden of "An Old Dyke's Tale" (see *Conditions: Six*), and to Patricia (Pat) Parker, "the fourth girl" of her family and so born "a threat"—that is, a poet, and unapologetically butch. I lived with *Conditions: Six* for two months before writing these poems. There were so many mothers writing in the collection, and so many missed or otherwise left-behind children. I wanted to let the mothers speak, as well as give the daughters a voice and perspective. What *Conditions: Six* taught me and what I hope my poems demonstrate is that love is; and life is contradictory, full of wonder, and vast. Second to this, *Conditions: Six* reiterated and reminded that shared womanhood does not equate to shared power or to shared victimhood. This offering on behalf of *Conditions*, in keeping with Pat Parker and in the words of Cheryl Clarke, "puts it on a very personal level" for me. Here's to herstory!

Cheryl R. Hopson received her PhD in English from the University of Kentucky in 2008. She is an associate professor of English and African American studies at Western Kentucky University in Bowling Green. Cheryl is a scholar and a poet and has published on womanist novelist Alice Walker, third-wave feminist writer and intellectual Rebecca Walker, and African American novelist, folklorist, and anthropologist Zora Neale Hurston—on whom she is writing a monograph. Cheryl's chapbooks *Fragile*

(2017) and *Black Notes* (2013) were published by Finishing Line Press. Her poems can be found in *The Toronto Quarterly, The Indianapolis Review, Not Very Quiet, Rise Up Review, DoveTales: Refugees and the Displaced*, and other venues. She claims, and is in gratitude of, Maya Angelou, Alice Walker, Audre Lorde, Barbara (*Home Girls*) Smith, June Jordan, Rebecca Walker, and Nikky Finney as artistic and life influences, and additionally credits "a long line of Black and going on women," to borrow from the late Lucille Clifton, and a few good men, for her love of the written word.

CONDITIONS: SEVEN

— Response by Amy Haejung

Object Series

Last weekend I ran into Helen. Or more accurately, I walked past Helen, in Prospect Park. I was making the rounds with my roommate's dog when I noticed her sitting on a bench further down the path. Even from a distance, and though it had been nearly three years since I'd last seen her, I recognized her almost immediately: the Supreme Object of Desire.

***

Lucy and I took to calling her ex-girlfriend's girlfriend "Helen" because she was the object of desire of an object of desire, the latter object being Lucy's ex. This was back in college, when we were in a mythological mood; we had decided to encrypt our love lives with codenames to conceal them from the general student body. But we couldn't think of an appropriate pseudonym for the ex, whom we temporarily referred to as "X."

Lucy liked the name Helen, but when I tried to name the ex "Paris," she protested that it wasn't typically Asian American enough. It was a ridiculous argument that went something like this:

"If we're committing to using these names, I want them to at least feel believable. I mean, have you ever heard of an Asian Paris?"

"London Tipton was almost named Paris. London is still Paris-adjacent."

"That was a TV show. A *kids'* TV show. And anyway, if we wanted to go by the myth, it would make more sense for Helen to be Paris and X to be Helen."

"But I'm used to calling Helen Helen. That would just be confusing."

By the end of this conversation, we agreed that maybe there was no single supreme object of desire, only many relative ones; and that maybe Helen was a lesbian and Paris was a woman, but all of them were white anyway and why should we apply their archetypes to our lives.

So we abandoned the theme and X remained X. We didn't change Helen's name, though.

***

For the next few weeks, Lucy talked about Helen until Helen sometimes replaced her in my dreams. She showed me updates on Helen's Instagram: pictures of X studying in her dorm room, pictures of X with pho, selfies with X and abominably clear skin. Neither of us had actually met Helen, but she had regardless become a fixture of Lucy's life and consequently mine.

Lucy said, "Fucking Helen and her thousand-ship face." The bitterness in her voice lodged inside me.

***

We graduated a couple months later, and mostly lost touch after the celebratory block party, where Lucy sad-drunk-kissed me, then sobbed and threw up behind some bushes for the rest of the evening because she saw Helen and X slow-dancing. I was crouching next to her, listlessly patting her back, trying to ignore the trace of sourness she left in my mouth. What power, I thought, and me with none of it, the sucker in this hierarchy of desire. When I turned again to her hunched form, I realized I felt no warmth, no weight; maybe I hadn't in a while. I stood up, told her I was going to bed, and left.

Maybe six months after that, Lucy reached out to tell me that things were finally going well with X and they were moving to

LA together. She said she wanted to get coffee with me before leaving, but it never happened.

***

Helen was talking to an older woman, well-dressed with short gray hair. When I neared them, Helen's eyes settled on my face for a brief moment, then flicked back indifferently. After I passed them I found I could no longer remember her real name.

Artist Statement

"Object Series," written for *Sinister Wisdom*'s tribute to *Conditions*, draws inspiration from three works published in *Conditions Seven* (1981): Rocky Gámez's excerpt from *The Gloria Stories*, Paula Gunn Allen's "Beloved Women," and Nellie Wong's "Asian American Women, Feminism and Creativity."

Amy Haejung lives in New York and works as a freelance copy editor and proofreader. She was selected as a finalist for the 2020 Kundiman Mentorship Lab in fiction. Her work has appeared in *Waxwing*.

CONDITIONS: EIGHT
— Response by Carmen Rios

Still Resonant, Conjuring Visions

"We expect change," co-founders Elly Bulkin, Rima Shore, and Jan Clausen declared in their introductory letter to *Conditions: Eight*. It shook me. It reminded me of the phrase I wrote in my diary one year after I came out: *i'm glad i changed.* I still am, ten years later; their letter, and the issue, reminded me why.

To say I feel *unmoored* by this moment—personally, politically, socially, culturally—is an understatement. While I write this, while I bury parts of myself in words and uncover others in the words of others, I am aware that the world outside is blazing, sometimes literally, with injustice and inhumanity. But I was also privileged enough to see the quarantine induced by the pandemic that gobbled up this year of our lives as an opportunity to transform, to heal, to reckon, to pause, to familiarize myself with myself. I committed to cocooning—to sitting still, to searching for myself in the silence, to resting so that I could store up enough energy to evolve.

When I turned thirty, I cast a humble spell for a rebirth. In July, five months into my own undoing-in-place, I lit a magic candle and asked for one more shot to get myself right. And then I opened *Conditions: Eight*, published eight years before I came screaming into the world, and found my way.

Inside *Eight*, I found my foremothers—standing in the sun, just like me, with their ears to heaven, waiting for a whisper of guidance while they try to decide which path to follow toward the light; standing on the outside looking in, just like me, with their eyes on the futures they reject, shimmering before them but somehow no longer feasible; standing close to their pain, just like me, with their hands stuck in the mess of it, so that they might begin to untangle and understand it. The "transitional issue" began with the introduction of a new collective of editors for the journal—Dorothy Allison, Cheryl Clarke, Jewelle L. Gomez, Carroll Oliver, Mirtha N. Quintanales, Rima Shore—and the feeling of an evolution permeated the entire bound collection. Each page was going to be a revelation, a revolution. I felt it calling to me once I opened it, and I could not put it down.

"Remember your past / and ours," ancestors command in Minnie Bruce Pratt's poem "Red String." "Always remember who you are." I have searched for this command throughout the last decade, hungry for ancestors of my own—for queer, mixed-race, messy women finding their own way and making up the steps so that I might follow. In *Eight* I found those I cherish and met even more.

Inside *Eight*, I found so many women articulating the kind of yearning nobody had ever instructed me to be aware of or advised me on how to manage: deep yearning for understanding an identity that transcends neat boxes or diatribes, that creates tension between where we come from and where we want to go, that forces us to make impossible decisions. I found Cherríe Moraga grappling with "passing" in the middle of a crisis of racial injustice and saw myself, too, in 2020, trying to decipher where I fit and who I needed to be in order to do the right thing during the Black Lives Matter uprisings; I found Hattie Gossett looking back on how little had changed for Black folks in America and then realized I now was doing the same, thirty-eight years later. Inside *Eight*, two writers—one a woman of color, the other a white woman and *Conditions* co-editor—reviewed the anthology *This Bridge Called My Back: Writings by Radical Women of Color*, the book that created a language with which I could begin to mend my own and go back to myself—a sacred text that remains resonant in a feminist movement where people like me, women who defy many boxes, still struggle to be seen and heard and understood.

"Certainly I . . . can attest to the terrible pain of being a bridge," Paula Gunn Allen writes in her review of *This Bridge*. "But I can also attest to the strength and clarity of commitment and vision that such a heritage engenders" (127). In her review, Jan Clausen remarks that the text "challenges *all* women 'to go further, to be more realistic,'" and "demonstrates that we can" (135).

I realize, for the first time, that I am not lost or caught between two places, two sites of my ancient belonging. I realize, for the first time, that instead I am right here in the thicket where they overlap, in a distinct place in which all of me and all of my contexts can belong at once, and that allowing myself to live there—to occupy a space, a series of identities, a number of questions that Clausen recognized then as rightfully "discomfiting"—can become an earthshaking act of rebellion in hindsight.

I close my eyes and think about Los Angeles, all my stuff in twelve boxes in the living room, the five years I'd already lost running across this sacred site of my own self-construction. I scribble in the margins: *did i come here to build my own world?* In my head, I make a note to write down all of the visions that will come to me next of what a world big enough to hold all the parts of me would look like.

Inside *Eight*, I found women searching for a home—for a sense of belonging inside their body, for the feeling of a community outside of their windows, for the elusive solace of knowing that they could honor the women who raised them while also defying the social order that had imprisoned them. In "El Paisano Is a Bird of Good Omen," Gloria Anzaldúa, in a piece from 1972, describes a young queer woman keeping her distance from a crowd on her own wedding day in the dry heat of *la tierra*, riding the fence that straddles the line between her freedom and her family. Chrystos's poem "Acrylic for Lee" cries out for the language of her father, which now can only be studied from books.

"This move has filled me up with questions," Barbara Smith writes in "Home," which I read while I shuttled myself back and forth to my new place, a tiny cottage with a front yard big enough for two strings of lights, the first place I would ever build my bed in that belonged only to me. "I want to tell someone who knew me long ago what we're doing," Smith continues. "I want her to know where I am" (101). I pick up the phone and call my mother, tell her I can't stop dancing in the middle of the single room with chapel ceilings, where I squeezed my bookcases into the corner and built by myself two closets from a box. I hang up and realize my yearning to go back to her is emerging from the fantasies that I am finally living in her stead.

All my mother has ever wanted is a place of her own, a dream that still eludes her because she chose me and my brother instead. I measure the walls to map out my furniture and realize that the world I'm building also belongs to her—because that is what she deserves for sharing her world with us, and because I do not know how to design my own future without leaving room for the parts of her I am determined to carry with me in our marches forward. I look down the line at every inch I've recorded in my sketchbook and whisper a prayer for my mother to find twice as many in this life for herself.

"She resolved not to endure the house," Pratt adds in "A Cold That Is Not the Opposite of Life," the final poem in her series in *Eight*, "but to live / in change, the cold to break at the bottom of the marsh, / the wind in the room to remind her / *There is something different from you dwelling here.*" I open the French doors where the spiders crawl in, lay in the dark on the white fur rug I carried across town in my car, and put on my mother's records.

Inside *Eight*, I found women demanding enough room to become themselves, demanding enough language to define themselves, demanding enough power to stand tall as themselves—insisting on their own paths in a world populated by millions of well-worn alternative ways to get to their destiny. In a review of Michelle Cliff's *Claiming an Identity They Taught Me To Despise*, Linda Hogan describes the narrator's transformation into "a woman who refuses any assimilation into a world she can't accept, who prefers to create her own strong self and name her identity." I underline the passage to remind myself that such refusal remains a possibility: *We build our own identities, families, future. We choose ourselves*, I write on a Post-it now stuck to the page. *We choose ourselves.*

I think about the desert on my way to and from the cottage, while the temperature rises outside the car doors and I watch Hollywood fade into the horizon line in the rearview mirror. Each time I get inside my tiny Chevy Spark, weary and exhausted from working, and push the gas pedal to carry my boxes farther east, a few steps closer to the Mojave, I feel myself coming back to life. When I open *Eight*, I find that I am not the only one standing in the sand staring out toward the sun in pursuit of herself. I find Sy Margaret Baldwin there, too, in the dry heat. "The desert is the background of who we are / the way only parts of us survive," she writes in one poem "The Desert Is Not the Enemy" (14). "In this remote place which has become my territory," she writes in another, "I thrive, loving what little there is" (12).

When I turned thirty, I didn't want to start over: I wanted to remember myself. I didn't want to run away: I wanted to go home again. I didn't want to go backwards: I wanted guidance in moving forward—in deliberately creating a life that it so often seemed nobody else had ever lived or tried to fathom. In *Eight*, I found a chorus of voices reminding me that I am not the only one who has repeated those prayers. In *Eight*, I saw the tangible evidence of such deliberation. "Says she reads, but is never specific what," Irena Klepfisz writes in one of the "Work Sonnets" in *Eight*:

Likes music, dancing. Smokes. Parties a lot, I think . . . Lives by herself. Thinks she should get married, but somehow can't bring herself to do it. "I like having the place to myself," she said the other day. Didn't specify what she was protecting. (82)

I feel less embarrassed after the piece, luxuriating in my solitude, building this church in which I can be devoted only to myself, and attempting to reconcile that with the isolation I have felt, despite my independence, throughout this moment. The pandemic pushed all of us away from each other, but my isolation comes not from the loss of romantic love but from failing to love myself—not from hours lost on Zoom calls while the world is on fire but from hours spent searching for stories that feel like my own. My isolation emerges from my parallel desires to stop performing in public for other people—to finally hear my own voice—and to stop concealing myself in private for fear the neighbors might find out who I am before I do. My isolation comes from realizing that sometimes I do not recognize myself.

"The lesbian writer does not have a monolithic room of her own," Bonnie Zimmerman asserts in her review of Elly Bulkin's *Lesbian Fiction: An Anthology* and *Lesbian Poetry: An Anthology* in *Eight* (144). Yet somehow, now I do—a small cottage in the back of the lot in Pasadena where I sit in the front yard surrounded by a wooden fence, absolutely alone and ecstatic about it, where I can pace back and forth and get to know myself.

When I put *Conditions: Eight* in its new place on my desk, facing the palm trees, I wonder if one day I will be on the other side of these pages—frozen in the past but still resonant, conjuring visions so large they stretch across generations instead of mere lifetimes—and if the other women who find me there will learn that once I stood here in the desert heat, wanting to cover my body in dust and dirt to remember where I came from, wanting to melt like clay so that I could reshape my life and maybe the entire world, and discover that they were never alone in their longing, either.

Carmen Rios has spent the last decade telling women's stories—including her own. She is currently the consulting digital editor at *Ms.* magazine and editorial director for The Jane Club and writes regularly for DAME, the Women's Media Center, and the National Women's History Museum. She is also co-founder of the Webby Award–nominated *Argot Magazine.* Carmen cut her teeth as a contributor at Everyday Feminism and Autostraddle's first-ever feminism editor, and her work has also appeared in BuzzFeed, *Bitch, Bust,* CityLab, ELIXHER, *Feministing, Feminist Formations,* GirlBoss, GrokNation, MEL, Mic, SIGNS, and the anthologies *WE SPOKE* and *Persistence is Resistance: Celebrating 50 Years of Gender, Women & Sexuality Studies.* You can follow her @carmenriosss and send fan mail at carmenfuckingrios.com.

CONDITIONS: NINE
— Response by SaraEllen Strongman

No More Nice Girls

Bonnie: (to Cheryl) *Could we be a little nice?*
Linda: No more nice girl.

The exchange above follows Cheryl Clarke and Jewelle Gomez's critiques of Toni Morrison's award-winning third novel *Song of Solomon* as having "so much garbage in it" and being full of "floating debris," respectively. These statements are shocking now but were even more so in 1983 in the still relatively early days of Black feminist criticism. Although Alice Walker's *The Color Purple* would win both the Pulitzer Prize and the National Book Award that year, there remained a reticence among Black women to publicly criticize Black women's writing. That the criticism appeared in *Conditions* meant the participants were airing their dirty laundry in front of outsiders (i.e. *white people, more specifically white women*). The contradictions and controversy of the "pentalog" (five-person conversation, so named by members of the conversation) "Black Women on Black Women Writers" in *Conditions: Nine* reflect the rapidly evolving nature of Black feminist criticism in the 1980s and the role that *Conditions* played in its growth and dissemination.

Although *Conditions* was founded by four white lesbians, it became a major site for the growth and articulation of Black (lesbian) feminist criticism. This was due in part to the founding editors' commitment to diversity; they understood the need to publish a racially and ethnically diverse group of authors and critics. In addition to drawing upon their personal networks to solicit work from women of color, the original *Conditions* collective handed over control of their fifth issue to co-editors Barbara

Smith and Lorraine Bethel. *Conditions: Five / The Black Women's Issue* brought together Black women's writing in a broad range of genres, from poetry to journal entries and critical essays. The essays in particular signaled the rapid growth of Black feminist criticism. In addition to essays on Black women's literature, and an essay on Black feminist therapy, Smith's contribution, "Notes for Yet Another Paper on Black Feminism, Or Will the Real Enemy Please Stand Up," built upon her previous work in "Toward a Black Feminist Criticism" (published in *Conditions: Two*) and took stock of the state of Black feminism in the present moment. Ultimately, *The Black Women's Issue* was the best-selling of all seventeen issues of *Conditions*. Subsequent issues continued to publish work—poetry, literary fiction, essays, and reviews—by women of color including Nellie Wong, Gloria Anzaldúa, Audre Lorde, Cherríe Moraga, Becky Birtha, and Bethel and Smith, among others.

In 1982, Bulkin, Clausen, and Shore decided to reorganize the editorial collective. Clausen left the collective after *Issue Eight* while Bulkin and Shore continued and were joined by five new members, including three Black women (Jewelle Gomez, Carroll Oliver, and Cheryl Clarke), one Latina (Mirtha N. Quintanales), and the only Southerner, Dorothy Allison. *Conditions: Nine* was the first issue published by this new multiracial editorial collective.

The new composition of the editorial collective generated new dynamics and tensions. Allison described attending the new collective's first meeting as an anxious occasion:

> They put together a mixed bunch of people who were not going to get along, and we had to work it out. I mean, I was suddenly working with Yankee black women, and they looked at me like, Who is this cracker? And I'm like, Ooh, they're going to eat me alive. . . . It was a hard transition to get to know each other, learn to trust each other. But we learned it doing the work and discovering that we all loved

the work and took the work entirely seriously. (Voices of Feminism Oral History Project, Smith College, https://www. smith.edu/libraries/libs/ssc/vof/transcripts/Allison.pdf.)

The contents of *Issue Nine* reflect the anxieties about this inclusive project both in the magazine and in the broader feminist movement, especially in feminist publishing. Other feminist journals, like *Heresies*, had been criticized for their failure to include the voices of women of color. Only a few years prior, the editorial board at *Chrysalis* had essentially imploded in part as a result of critiques of the magazine's handling of race. Would the newly assembled editorial collective be able to work together successfully? Or would personal and systemic challenges stymie their vision for the magazine? In particular, the conversation "Black Women on Black Women Writers," among Jewelle Gomez, Cheryl Clarke, Evelynn Hammonds, Bonnie Johnson, and Linda Powell, reflects the changes that had taken place in the larger feminist movement, and in multiracial and Black feminist movements in particular, in the years since *Conditions: One* (1977).

While the editors of *Conditions: Five* in 1978 and 1979 had struggled to secure submissions from Black women, and Shockley, in her review essay, had only been able to identify a handful of Black lesbian writers currently publishing, by 1983 the landscape of Black women's writing and Black feminist criticism was much changed. By then Kitchen Table Press was operating and *Azalea*, a journal of third world lesbian writing, had been publishing for several years. By 1983, three major anthologies had featured the work of Black and women of color feminists: *Home Girls*, an expanded version of *Conditions: Five*, edited by Smith; *This Bridge Called My Back: Writings by Radical Women of Color* (Anzaldúa and Moraga, eds., 1982); and *But Some of Us Are Brave: Black Women's Studies*. All three volumes are discussed in the pentalog. But the primary venues for the publication of Black feminist writing were still publications founded (and frequently headed) by white women.

The pentalog voices the anxieties and joys of a Black feminist criticism in the early 1980s, especially within white spaces. In the introduction, Clarke describes the inspiration for the conversation as deriving from the "ambivalence" they all felt about their work as Black feminist critics—both how they might impose a Black feminist framework onto all Black women's writing and how their work, published in white feminist publications, exposed themselves, and all Black women, to the prying eyes of "outsiders." Clarke frames the conversation as an attempt to work through the "dilemma" of exposing "family secrets" and reveals that they attempted "to create an atmosphere of anything can be said" during the taping to combat their urge to self-censor. The conversation tackles this question as well as other topics like "lesbian as aesthetics and politics" and "the literary tradition of black women." What plays in this conversation is a shared attempt to limn the contours of a developing tradition. As Linda Powell notes, "What we're doing is a new bird."

Rather than presenting a unified, internally coherent vision of Black feminist criticism and art, the participants in the pentalog openly critique other Black women writers. The conversation is threaded through with anxieties and ambiguities. Although Gomez and Clarke criticize *Song of Solomon*, Powell names it as one of her five favorite novels. There is also tension between the excitement these women feel about the growing availability of writing by Black women and their frustration with its quality and how the tokenization of Black women's literature seems to limit its growth. (The logic among mainstream publishers, it seemed, was that one book, one author was sufficient.) At the same time that the participants rejoiced at each new title authored by a Black woman, they refused to stay complacent. Their joy at the increasing availability of books by and about Black women did not prevent them from criticizing the work of Black women writers. Most severely judged are bell hooks, Ann Allen Shockley, and literary scholar Deborah McDowell.

"We're at a new place because there *is* a black feminist criticism. We don't have to start by justifying our existence," Evelynn Hammonds says. The participants regarded Smith's "Towards a Black Feminist Criticism" and Alice Walker's "In Search of Our Mother's Gardens" as the first foray into this new field. Although both Walker's and Smith's now canonical essays had been presented at academic conferences—Walker's at Radcliffe and Smith's at Howard—the pentalog took place outside of the ivory tower. The line between scholarship and criticism in Black feminist thought is often blurred because many Black feminist critics are also academics. But Black feminism had a robust life entirely outside of the academy. While Black feminism certainly found nourishment inside the ivory tower, much Black feminist theorizing happened elsewhere, including in the pages of *Conditions*.

Also at issue in this conversation were the consequences of critique for the participants' personal lives. Although it was growing, the community of Black feminists, especially Black lesbian feminists, was still relatively small. The relationships between Black feminists were precious. Barbara and Beverly Smith's piece "'I Am Not Meant to be Alone and Without You Who Understand': Letters from Black Feminists" in *Conditions: Four* attested to the importance of the connections between Black women in nurturing Black feminist theory and helping often-isolated Black feminists survive the day-to-day trials of living in a racist, homophobic, and sexist society. Clarke describes her dilemma as a critic this way: "The question becomes for me in many cases not, 'What am I to say?' but rather, 'Can I say what I need to say and still keep my friendships?'" Like Clarke, Black feminists struggled to balance the rigor of their analysis with their desire for community. Indeed, Audre Lorde penned a letter, published in *Conditions: Ten*, critiquing the pentalog, which she felt contained "personal attacks" and produced "destruction" rather than an assessment of the current state of Black women's writing as the title promised.

Placing the pentalog alongside the other contents of the issue further illuminates the controversy it courted. *Conditions: Nine* also contains reviews of two major Black feminist texts: Lorde's biomythography *Zami* and the anthology *All the Women Are White, All the Men Are Black, But Some of Us Are Brave: Black Women's Studies* (Barbara Smith, Patricia Bell-Scott, and Akasha (Gloria) Hull, eds., 1982.) Clarke had written a very critical review of *But Some of Us Are Brave* for *Sinister Wisdom*. She and other participants in the pentalog had a much more nuanced view of the anthology than the *Conditions* review espoused. Both in the pentalog and *Conditions: Nine* as a whole, we see a Black feminist canon in formation and just how rich and varied Black feminist criticism was at this moment.

SaraEllen Strongman is an assistant professor of Afroamerican and African Studies at the University of Michigan, Ann Arbor. She researches and writes about Black feminisms, Black women's political and cultural history, and African American literature. Her manuscript in progress, *The Sisterhood: Black Women, Black Feminism, and the Women's Liberation Movement*, examines the moment when black women began calling themselves "Black feminists" during the 1970s and 1980s. Specifically, she argues that the work of a cohort of black women critics, poets, and writers laid the groundwork for what we now know as Black feminist thought. Her work has been published in *Feminist Theory* and is forthcoming in *Feminist Studies*.

CONDITIONS: TEN

Shromona Mandal
Vienna, VA 22180

August 24th, 2020

Conditions
P.O. Box 56,
Van Brunt Station,
Brooklyn, N.Y. 11215

Dear Conditions Editorial Collective: Dorothy Allison, Elly Bulkin, Cheryl Clarke, Nancy Clarke Otter, Adrienne Waddy

SUBJECT: Gratitude for what 1984 has given me in 2020

    I'm reaching out to cordially invite you, the editorial collective, to step out of 1984 and into the future. In year 2020, I find myself, a 21-year-old Bengali lesbian caught in the tangle of fascism in the so-called United States and the country on my passport, India. I'm writing simultaneously from inside a global pandemic that has shut down borders and amongst widespread uprisings to defend Black lives. In between the 2020 pandemic and uprisings, the USPS is on the brink of being shut down after being gutted by legislation and the Amazon online retail empire. Regrettably, the only letters I've mailed are to the State Department and the IRS and one postcard from New York to Bangkok. Until now. I commit my first real letter to Conditions— a feminist magazine of writing by women, with an emphasis on writing by lesbians, issue Ten, 1984.

    My copy of Conditions: Ten passed down from one "Judith Barrington, Portland, OR" was mailed to me from Julie R. Enszer, (you will know her as the unstoppable editor of Sinister Wisdom and one of the most ardent keepers of our herstories). Thank you both! Passed between the hands of these women, from press to post to shelf, this copy of the issue is alive and well in my hands. I've been putting its 36-year-old pages to good use with several colored pens in an attempt to match Ann Cammett's energy. Her cover for this issue is so bold and confrontational. The cover is red and white with rows of "CONDITIONS" stacked on top of the word "TEN" divided by a faux torn-edge design with relief prints marking the transitions between sections waiting to be decoded. From font to design, Ann Cammett anticipated the future all too well. For you in 1984 she was ushering in the succinct, text heavy design era of type and print in her decade. For me in 2020, she was setting us up for the reprisal of the retro 80's typography style that characterizes our online political spaces today.

During the 2020 coronavirus pandemic, we are cut off from the shared communal forums where we circulated our ideas. My generation instead anxiously shares thousands of cool, bold, and high contrast text-essays on the social media platform called Instagram. Ever since March, we have used Instagram's little squares on our phone screens loaded with rhetoric, facts, theories, and humor to attract and generate conversations about justice in a moment of mass death. Here lies an integral lesson from Conditions: Ten, even our graphics on Instagram have been handed down to us, just like the poetics and politics within the pages of the issue. From cover to cover and at the turn of each page, is the pulse of a healthy community sustained by the editorial collective and the assemblage of women who wrote for Conditions: Ten.

I am stuck within the four walls of my childhood bedroom due to the pandemic, yet Conditions: Ten transports me to Brooklyn, 1984 with the letter "To Our Readers:" where the women of the editorial collective were contending with: 1. the New York State Council on the Arts which rejected the collective's grant application for funding due to the observation that the magazine was too lesbian to be literature; 2. the transition of losing four and gaining two new editorial collective members; 3. the collective celebrating their banner for the 20th Anniversary for the March on Washington; and

4. organizing readings in the "Artists' Call Against US Intervention in Central America." As a political organizer, I have been curious about but mostly unable to make space for collectively making art as a form of organizing. Yet here was Conditions: Ten, leading me to one such moment from the very start, where the editorial collective used their literary knowledge, together with their network of writers and readers, to build political power through poetic skills.

I am currently an undergraduate senior in a setting where writing feels like busywork for grades and a rat-race for original analysis, a competition for the next smartest paper. Through reading the pages of Conditions: Ten and writing for this tribute, I began to learn the ways that intentional, ambitious, and small-scale circulations can do the heavy lifting of building power. Instead of studying theory to deconstruct as I do in the undergraduate world, I am reading Conditions: Ten to find a community across time and space — writers to build ideas with, lessons to learn without a grade — hand in hand. A clear example of the non-academic, community-based analytical goals of Conditions: Ten is a review from one of its celebrity writers — Judith Butler. The issue features Butler's 1983 review of "The Politics of Reality" by Marilyn Frye, where Butler critiques Frye's ideas as an "academic elite," whose writing framed patriarchy and the sexual oppression of womanhood from the singular point of view of white women's victimhood (p. 162). Fast forward to 2020 and Judith Butler is probably one of the most infamously inaccessible academics, yet her work published in this issue remains a testament to Conditions' community building-power.

Butler's critique brings me to the core of Conditions: Ten that makes it an immortal time capsule on print community and power-building: its reviews. The reviews published in these issues are precious exercises of literary, poetic, and community conversations for all of us to read and learn from. An example is Jo Cochran's visceral admiration for Joy Harjo's poetry in her review of She Had

Some Horses. Cochran is moved deeply by Harjo's lyric poem "Alive" and writes, "From within myself I react and understand these lines, this song. I would like to find in myself this woman who is free to sing and cross lines," (p. 174). This review pulls me into the intense and intimate moment shared by two Indigenous women in conversation. Throughout her review, Cochran also capaciously cites several Indigenous women poets and their knowledges as she locates herself and Harjo's poetry within this abundant landscape. The generosity with which Cochran writes this review is more than just a citational practice. For me, Cochran not only builds me a library of Indigenous women's poetry, but also gives us a lesson in empathy and in bearing witness.

Cheryl Clarke's review of Keeper of Accounts by Irena Klepfisz also generously teaches me what to do with the words of women when differences in time, history, and experience "[create] barriers to my relationship with [them]," (p. 154). Reading both the poetry which relays intergenerational trauma and its review which unfolds the mechanics of empathy, I witness an exchange between two incredible women – a Jewish elder and a Black elder. In a note I scribbled on the last page, I realize that I've found an embodiment of trust. One where the three of us, reading and writing from our little pockets, come together in pages — bound to each other. Even when, and perhaps especially when, Clarke carefully interprets that Klepfisz "gives us no visions of a future free of danger or repression," all three of us are meeting each other at a place of vulnerability and political uncertainty, in 1984 and in 2020.

Regaling in the intimacy within the newfound format of women writing reviews of each other's work, I devoured the poems and essays in Conditions: Ten with renewed purpose and intention. Reading the poetry from Toi Derricotte, Luzma Umpierre, Christina Peri Rossi and her translator Patrice Titterington, Sy Margaret Baldwin, Willyce Kim, Chrystos, Honor Moore, Enid Dame, and Marilyn Hacker felt like the opposite of dreaming. Instead, their words were meditations for every inch of my body and mind. The poems thread together the daily memories, mundane motions, routine emotions, and faithful Sapphic fantasies of these women and the women from their communities. The intimacy in the poems is not soft — it is firm and threatening if crossed. An example that stands out for me is Enid Dame's unyielding poem "Ethel Rosenberg: A Sestina," written with both grief and exasperation to the political dissident executed by the U.S. government: "You've been dead most of my life. I'm the type of woman / who questions what's easy. At night, with crystal and table, / I beg ghosts out of dead revolutions to come to me, to talk sense" (p. 104).

So when the New York State Council of the Arts rejected the grant application from the Conditions editorial collective, it was obviously not because the publication was "too lesbian to be literature." It was because the heady sense of love and revolution is a dangerous craft passed down by the women writing poetry for liberation. In Conditions: Ten, each poem is either a transistor, a transformer, or a capacitor in a circuit buzzing with the electricity of revolution, whether explicitly named or not. I was electrified.

That electric sensation of revolution and love also poured over into the essays and fiction in Conditions: Ten. I am used to reading essays. Personal essays are where I found agency during my freshman year of college. The writers in this issue expand on that sense of agency and efficacy, reconnecting me to the pleasures of the genre. In "Hard Ground: Jewish Identity, Racism, and Anti-Semitism," by Elly Bulkin and "Granny, Mama, Carrie, Bell: Race and Class, A Personal Accounting" by Mab Segrest rallied me as both writers explain the complicated political reality grounding their lesbian literary work and the liberatory visions they are building as intergenerational organizers struggling against racism, classism, and anti-Semitism.

Short fiction written by and about lesbians was not something I had really encountered or knew existed outside of the online fanfictions I read throughout high school[1]. Until now. When I started reading Sinister Wisdom, the journal which led me to Conditions, I found the type of drama I had been yearning for within its short fiction pieces. Needless to say, I was looking forward to the short fiction in Conditions: Ten and cherish what I have found. Andrea Freud Lowenstein's "Crab Queen" was memorable in its hilarity but also its honesty. Freud expertly writes the story of a rural Christian straight woman whose already chaotic life is turned upside down when her lesbian academic sister visits home with her girlfriend in tow. I wonder, jokingly, whether the story will parallel a scene in my future when the news of my lesbianism will inevitably invade my ancestral village in Rasulpur, West Bengal when I visit the many Dadu and Dida [2] part of my extended family.

Barbara Banks's "About the Lizards" is a story exploring the moment when the son of a Black lesbian witnesses the multitudes of his mother's life: e.g. the fragile and intersectional space straddled by a Black woman mourning both a husband and a Pan Africanist movement but who now leans on the love and support of

---

1 Online fanfictions are multi-chapter stories or short vignettes written by young queer and trans people. Authors take characters who should have been written as gay lovers or as queer characters but were canonically written as straight from compelling fictional universes (like Harry Potter or Avatar the Last Air-bender). Writers put characters in fictional fan-created scenarios and stories. They are usually posted on websites such as Archive of Our Own under anonymous usernames which are sanctuaries from intellectual property right regimes.

---

2 The Bengali term for "grandfather" and "grandmother" used to refer to all elderly members of the family.

a white woman to survive all colliding with each other. The short fiction in this issue carved out the space that I have been craving from fiction in general – a space where the dilemmas of our communities and movements, clearly cyclical and unsolved, are tended to.

Another important way in which Conditions: Ten strengthened community and sharpened its analysis through care was via conversations generated by letters to the editorial collective. Although my letter to the collective is saturated with admiration from the point of view of a student of the publication, I appreciate the letter Audre Lorde wrote in response to Conditions Nine which is published at the end of this issue. Audre Lorde opens her letter to the magazine by addressing the discussion of Black lesbian aesthetics between Cheryl Clarke, Jewelle Gomez, Evelynn Hammonds, Bonnie Johnson, and Linda Powell in "Conversations and Questions: Black Women on Black Women Writers." Lorde describes the piece as a pentalog that "veered off" and "left much to be desired." Lorde observed that the dialogues devolved from practicing Black feminist criticism to criticizing Black lesbian writers "in terms of personal attack [...] to demolish any pretense of a constructive examination" of their work (p. 178). While Lorde calls in the writers for an unsuccessful attempt at criticism, her letter simultaneously articulates what Black feminist criticism could and ought to be, modeling the very practice it is advocating.

I was so excited reading Audre Lorde's response because it displays what conflict within a healthy community looks like – a generous engagement as opposed to the cold and cut-off act of subtweeting on the internet[3] Just as Lorde names that "criticism [...] is a learned art," writing letters to confront conflict, publishing letters by the criticized party for the reader to ruminate on, and

3 Subtweeting refers to writing posts on the social media platform Twitter that are criticizing something or someone without directly addressing them or notifying them to avoid confrontation

learning from confrontation are learned skills. Looking forward to my life in 2020, I am in the process of flushing out principles and practices with a coalition of student organizers trying to rid our campus of policing. With three years of intense and explosive experiences in student organizing, I and others in our organizations are coming to the table with a commitment to never avoid conflict and to treat all conflict with care. In other words, making a commitment to fight with and for each other. In her letter, Audre Lorde, whose work and life are studied deeply by prison and police abolitionists, has put a moment of healthy conflict to words. I thank you for publishing it. It has given me the courage to write and to organize with vulnerability and honesty. Skipping ahead, I am also grateful for the thoughtful and reflective response from the editorial collective to Audre Lorde's letter published in the following issue of Conditions.

This brings me back to Conditions: Ten as a whole. You, the editors and the writers whom you have published, have my immense gratitude for giving me something precious. When reading Conditions: Ten, I witnessed and took refuge in 1984 when lesbianism was forging transnational links and building a different type of coalition. It is this work that scaffolds all the ways I understand and experience my life in its entirety. Thanks to you all who put your blood, sweat, and tears into this issue despite all of the financial and political conditions at the time of this publication. I have been able to find—all within this pandemic and these uprisings— what it means to be a non-voting, temporary immigrant lesbian with an unraveling relationship to Bengali, upper-caste womanhood. And as precious as this issue is, so is the motivation that Conditions: Ten gives me to write. This issue has reached across time and space to encourage me to make mistakes and to correct them. I am eager to have my submissions accepted or rejected, but especially edited. This is important to me. As I write you this letter from 2020, I am reminded that I arrived at Conditions:

Ten because it was passed down to me by Julie and
Judith. Your work in 1984, as captured by the name
"Conditions" and your ongoing work in 2020 signal that
conditions don't just account for the tangible reality,
but also how these conditions feel, how the material of
our present resonates, and what we can create together,
intergenerationally.

Fighting with my back to yours,
Shromona Mandal (they/them)

    P.S. If you somehow end up reading this in 1984,
don't throw away the Classified Ads. Somewhere in 2020,
you could sell them to collectors online as vintage posters!

CONDITIONS: ELEVEN/TWELVE
— Response by Barrie Jean Borich

We Live in History Differently: On Conditions Eleven/Twelve

I don't remember when or where I first saw an issue of *Conditions*, but I started reading the magazine in the early 1980s, while in my early twenties. I was a still-forming queer woman who'd left the industrial realms of Chicago to reinvent myself. Now I see I was considering my geography, my class, my whiteness, and the forms of my desires, though at the time all I knew was that I was trying to shake off an unnameable chokehold. I first remember reading the magazines in my terrible-beautiful old upstairs duplex in South Minneapolis, the same apartment where I fell in love with a woman for the first time. I was working for a small semi-collective feminist theater company, writing publicity copy. I'd had sex with a few women, pined after a few more, but it was in this apartment where I studied these little lesbian magazines and made the full turn, my new lover . . . and me with the dark curly hair and I huddling in bed, cringing and laughing, while the telephone rang and rang, my last cis-male lover—calling frantically even though he knew I didn't pick up because I was finally doing what we'd both known I was preparing to do: leave him for a woman.

My last year in the apartment was the year *Conditions: Eleven/Twelve/The Double Issue* (1985) came out. Reading through it again now, thirty-five years later, I am struck by the formative picture it provides of the atmosphere of my life back then—not who I was yet, fully, but the human I aspired to be. So many of the stories in *Conditions* were about women finally leaving men for woman lovers, women breaking away from abuse, women grappling with racism, poverty, government. So many of the poems were about bars, bodies, politics, sexual violence, addiction, lust. So many of the essays and reviews were passionate and accessible works of first-person political theory. There has been no other time in my life, including graduate school and years of teaching in creative writing programs, where what I was reading, writing, creating in my workplace, and discussing with my friends was all part of a common and evolving fabric.

That wreck of an apartment—it probably should have been condemned, but then seemed to me luxuriously spacious—had a living room where I'd hung frayed lace tablecloths over the windows and placed the large round end of a telephone wire spool, set on cinder blocks, in the center. My friends from the theater, mostly lesbians (if not yet, then soon to be), gathered around that table, sitting on swaying chairs I'd bought for a few bucks at one of those old junk stores that used to everywhere, laughing and getting high but also talking through all we believed and desired. My bed was a futon on the ground in the middle room of the circular apartment, my desk a door on cinder blocks set in a sunny alcove corner overlooking the street. I used an electronic typewriter, the kind with that tiny, one-line computer screen, to revise poems, a couple of which I would publish in little feminist journals in coming years, and many more I would discard. Mostly what I was doing then was educating myself. I read articles by sex-positive and anti-racist lesbian-feminist theorists, and on yellow legal pads wrote drafts of poems and long letters to friends back in Illinois. I had dropped out of college at twenty and spent the next half-decade putting together another kind of education altogether, key to the writer I am today, and the literary magazines I read—*Sinister Wisdom*, *Heresies*, and *Conditions*—were my core curriculum.

The names in *Conditions: Eleven/Twelve* alone form an extraordinary list: Dorothy Allison, Cheryl Clarke, Joy Harjo, Judith McDaniel, Sapphire, Valerie Miner, Cherríe Moraga, Samuel Ace (under his previous name), Shay Youngblood, Amber Hollibaugh, Joan Nestle, and Barbara Smith, to name a few—in addition to reviews of books by Michelle Cliff, Jan Clausen, and Audre Lorde.

This was the era in which Audre Lorde published *Zami* and Cherríe Moraga published *Loving in the War Years*, books that formed me the way other writers talk about being formed by Montaigne or Proust or Woolf, but it would be close to a decade before Dorothy Allison published *Bastard Out of Carolina*, Joan Nestle published *A Persistent Desire*, and Sapphire published *Push*, and twenty-five years before Joy Harjo became the US Poet Laureate. Most of these writers' major books were still ahead of them, and according to my searches, today a majority of even the lesser-known writers, if they are still among the living, are teaching or retired from teaching in universities across the country. Here on the pages of journals like *Conditions* the foundations of a living community aesthetic were forming, freshly and sentence-by-sentence.

Rereading in 2020, page-by-page, from poem to story, to essay, to review, to the list of books received, to the classifieds, to ads for other journals, books, bookstores, and lesbian-run editorial services—all the hallmarks of politically engaged literary journals going back to early twentieth-century magazines like *The Masses* and the *Little Review*—I am transported back to a time, long before I was an academic, when I wasn't reading and writing for any reason other than to find a space for all the desires I was still then just discovering, an ethos that combined queer sex and feminism with direct and sonically beautiful sentences, narratives that described as well as critiqued, and arguments that did not suppress but did build upon the different ways we all live in history—a multiracial theoretical base called *intersectional* today, but then was understood as intuitively pushing through the heady combination of both self-invention and difference.

Joan Nestle's stunning essay-review in this issue about the three-author anthology *Yours in Struggle: Three Feminist Perspectives on Anti-Semitism and Racism*, by Elly Bulkin, Minnie Bruce Pratt, and Barbara Smith, is an example of the nonfiction in these magazines. More forthcoming and vulnerable than even Baldwin, there were few precursors to these yokes of distinct poetic and narrative descriptive voice with memoiristic revelation and sharp, queer political thinking. The *Conditions* essayists, individually and collectively, invented a new form of first-person nonfiction a decade before literary memoir was reborn in mainstream literary circles and the term "creative nonfiction" started to show up in university creative writing curriculums. These writers, and many others who published their early work in *Conditions*, created a new form of the essay, but rarely (one exception being in my own writings about the history of nonfiction literary form) get much credit. Nestle describes Black lesbian feminist Barbara Smith's ethical essaying and then practices the form herself, declaring her position as a white American Jewish lesbian, writing:

> [Barbara Smith] ducks no issues and claims no false purity for herself. She writes with the need to clear the air, to get some things said and then let's get on with it. . . . We have lived in history differently, Blacks and Ashkenazi Jews. Surely we can respect this difference without losing title to our own pain. There has been and is enough hell for both of us, but as a white Jew I see the places Jews can go and Blacks cannot. I see where the guns are pointed and who has refuge and who has not. (211–12)

There is much in today's QTIPOC and intersectional feminist conversation that is missing in these early 1980s works. Trans and genderqueer lives are not yet visible in these theoretical attempts. The concept of gender differences between queer women, a change in the conversation pioneered first in literary magazines by Amber Hollibaugh, Cherríe Moraga, and Joan Nestle—the seeds of my own second coming-out as a queer femme—had just begun to emerge in lesbian discourse. Judith Butler had not even published her paradigm-smashing *Gender Trouble* yet, and one issue earlier, in the 1984 *Conditions: Ten*, Butler published a review of Marilyn

Frye's essays describing herself in her bio (three years before publishing her own first book) as an "aspiring theorist." So much thinking still awaited invention. From today's point of view, we can see the limits of building a liberation movement solely on the intersections of sexual desire and a fixed gender binary, and today social media is crowded with the battles around what I consider this key error of lesbian-feminist analysis (including my own). However, mid-1980s radical ways of thinking about bodies and identities saved countless lives, even if core theoretical omissions, and the belief by some that queer knowledge is finite, obscure some of the still-necessary inventions by that era's most fluid lesbian thinkers.

Whether remembered or not, the deep antiracist commitment to both personalized discourse and intimate struggle over understanding of structural power found on the pages of *Conditions* set the ground for today's interrogations. The kind of writing we still need in order to theorize the place of all our bodies in history started, in part, here. We would not be going too far to say that *Conditions* was at the center of a Brooklyn-based Queer Women's Renaissance with an underground national reach, in the same ways the magazine *Fire!!* was the flashpoint of the Harlem Renaissance in New York, the magazine *Negro Story* and the South Side Community Art Center were the gathering points of the Chicago Black Renaissance, and the mimeo journal *Beatitude* and City Lights Bookstore helped create the San Francisco Renaissance of North Beach Beats. *Conditions* and other little queer magazines of its time deserve study comparable to that of other turning-point moments of American cultural production.

I had yet to publish when I first read *Conditions* while inviting so many new ways of thinking into my head and my bed. During my time in that disheveled apartment, my subsistence-pay day-job work shifted from feminist theater to multicultural small press publishing, and my love life expanded from one woman lover to two, nonmonogamy one of the feminist theories I tried, but regretfully failed to make work for long in my own life. In a couple years I'd have a new apartment, meet the love of my femme-butch genderqueer married life, shift from poetry to creative nonfiction, and go back to school to meld the most radical university education I could muster to my underground, autodidactic degree in the lesbian little magazines. The man who rang my phone that sunny Sunday morning has since passed away, and the Minneapolis duplex where I lived, as well as the one next door where he lived, have been torn down and taken away; phones don't even ring the same way anymore. I lived in that apartment before I had a credit card, and the address doesn't even show up on my credit report, so I can't use the Internet to prove that time in my life even happened. My only receipts are lesbian word-of-mouth, from the woman in bed with me that morning who still lives in Minneapolis with the love of her life. Our survival and self-creation take many forms and I have carried one source, those magazines, with me, between apartments and cities, for decades, their practices and editorial reach core to my own literary magazine editing, and my teaching on the history of little magazines. When I'm stuck, while writing my own essays and books, I fall back on what I learned from the writers of the *Conditions* era, which is to clearly state my thinking and my desire, then allow the intimate conditions of curiosity, uncertainly, love, struggle, and justice-seeking itself to carry my text forward.

Barrie Jean Borich is the author of *Apocalypse, Darling*, which *PopMatters* said "soars and seems to live as a new form altogether. It's poetry, a meditation on life as 'the other,' creative nonfiction, and abstract art." Her memoir *Body Geographic* won a Lambda Literary Award, and her book-length essay *My Lesbian Husband* won the Stonewall Book Award. Borich is a professor at DePaul University where she directs the interdisciplinary LGBTQ Studies minor and edits *Slag Glass City*, a journal of the urban essay arts.

conditions
conditions
conditions

a feminist magazine

We are concerned that women's/lesbian publications have often failed to reflect the experiences and viewpoints of Third World, working-class and older women. CONDITIONS includes work in a variety of styles by both published and unpublished writers of many different backgrounds. We welcome submissions from all women who feel that a commitment to other women is an integral part of their lives.

CONDITIONS, INC.
BOX 56
VAN BRUNT STATION
BROOKLYN, NY 11215

CONDITIONS: THIRTEEN
— Response by Rachel Afi Quinn

Afi Is for Us

"We too have been taught forgetting," writes Abena Busia in her poem "Achimota: From the Story My Mother Taught Me," published in *Conditions: Thirteen* (1986) some thirty-five years ago. I was surprised to find her words here, to recognize another a Ghanaian feminist scholar between the pages of this lesbian publication. I was equally delighted to meet her in this place of knowing—a place of sharing grief and loss tied to African diasporic memory. As Busia notes, "We are schooled in another language now / and names lose their meanings except / as labels. / We are being taught forgetting" (95). Her poem, published in part one of two International Issues of *Conditions*, joins other women's stories that are as much about memory as they are about lives lived well beyond the boundaries of the United States and about the transnational nature of the publication's Brooklyn-based feminist community. This particular issue of *Conditions* archives a series of moments for readers to cling to, of places we may have been, places that have shaped us, and glimpses into the faraway places that have made the people we love; we encounter in the text details that have indelibly marked those we hope to know intimately.

Busia's "Achimota" is a *punctum*, a hole, a tear in the fabric, "a cast of the dice" as Roland Barthes described it in *Camera Lucida* (27). Her poem emerged from the pages of *Conditions* for me with the familiarity of a life once lived—or at least the curiosity of a path not taken. In her 2016 oral history for the Women's Learning Partnership Archive of the Global Women's Movement (https://learningpartnership.org/resource/abena-busia-oral-history-audio-files), Busia shares her childhood memories of leaving

Ghana after the ousting of her father, Prime Minister Kofi Abrefa Busia (1969–72). With her poem, she takes us back to Ghana: "There is a place between Accra and the Legon hills / where they built the famous school." Achimota is a location that she can point to with certainty, across generations, one that determines social status and the value of education among our people.

As it happens, several of my oldest siblings—out of the thirteen who grew up in Ghana—spent their formative years at that boarding school. Sent to Smith and Vassar and Yale in the 1980s, they became part of the "brain drain" that Ghana would experience. It shaped who they are today, opened doors, determined trajectories, determined who among them would go study and make their lives in the United States. As one of the country's highest markers of educational privilege of that era, "A-chi-*mo*-ta" was a name often stated with pride, the word a rhythm. Achimota means "speak no name" in Ga, the most commonly spoken language in Ghana's capital, Accra.

***

My first visit to Ghana was when I was seventeen years old. I watched as a silent young man cooked lunch in great big pots in the kitchen of my auntie's house. As he reached for the handle of a wooden spoon, I could see that he had my very same enormous hands and long fingers.

"Is he . . . ? Is he related to me?" I asked.

"A second cousin," my auntie confirmed, though she never introduced me to him.

Ghana was the first time I was surrounded by pieces of myself. As unfamiliar as I was with Ghanaian culture at that point, I had lived my entire life in a body marked by this faraway place. Tentatively I began claiming my father's culture as my own, while my Ghanaian relatives began enthusiastically claiming *me*. They called me by my middle name "Afi," giving it sound and meaning that it had never had before. It is a day name; I am a Friday-born. I am an Ewe, I learned. I am the only one of my father's children with a white American mother, yet, I am told, I most resemble my Ewe grandmother Nano, who was fair in color. Like my older sister Mercy, I have Nano's cheekbones and long jawline, but Mercy's skin is much darker than my own. When they see me, a "Yevu" or "white" in their midst, come home for a visit, they recognize me too. When I went with my older brother Kofi to our family's village in the Volta Region, I could see the intimacies of my family's gene pool. People we greeted for the first time that day were obviously blood-related strangers. In them, I recognized my brothers' smiles, my sisters' eyes, my own long arms, my grandmother's high cheekbones. Walking through Akutukope, around each corner that I turned, they called out to me beyond greetings and across language barriers. "Nano!" they shouted, claiming me.

Years later, it is my grandfather—my late grandfather's brother, in fact—known as Teacher, who notices. Staring down at my sandals in the dirt, he remarks, "Don't ever let your father tell you that you aren't his child. You have those same big toes that all the Glover women have." I smile at these moments of being claimed. My big toes had always seemed to look funny to people in the other places I've lived. I loved him then, for recognizing me in such a tangible way, and for looking closely. Teacher (pronounced "Teacha") had once explained to my mother that I must change my last name to that of my father because, he insisted, "Afi is for us!" My brother Emmanuel and I, to this day, have a good laugh about Teacha's obstinate demand that I am a child earned by my father's entire family: "Afi is for us!" he repeated, while sending his wife to get straws for our sodas with little more than the wave of his hand. I wondered then to whom I really did belong, though I had no interest in being the property of another. My Jewish American mother points out that she was the one who had done all the work in raising me and had paid for all of my education, but somehow her claims on me had never been this strong. Yet my Ghanaian relatives knew so little about me still—about my queerness or my interests or my studies—and I remain unsettled by their gendered sense of entitlement.

I was one of those private school–educated, mixed-race Black kids who grew up in a liberal, progressive multicultural world dominated by whiteness. Born and raised in Durham, North Carolina, my earliest identity was formed within white middle-class neighborhoods, college towns, and other spaces of educational privilege. I began my adolescent journey of self-discovery in a sea of people who looked nothing like me and struggled to see me outside of the messages they held dear about Black people in the U.S. South. I held few stories about Ghana until I went there for the first time before my senior year of high school. Up until then, I hardly knew my family in Ghana or all the siblings that I had (only having met a few). I sought out my own story because it had not been given to me, and the exoticized privilege that my mixedness awarded me with was never going to be enough. I am one of those brown people welcomed by whiteness, who pleasantly surprises for being culturally similar enough—I am safe enough. Did I feel most at home in a white landscape? It was all I knew.

"You don't look like a Rachel," a Black boy told me in third grade, "you look more like an April." And I tried to rename myself too, the way my older sister had in high school when her Old Testament name wasn't cool—which is to say it wasn't Black enough for her peers. Did I realize as an adolescent that no one in the movies I watched looked like me? Being invisibilized by white supremacy, chided by white liberalism, and under constant pressure to assimilate surely contributed to my many stints of depression and endless feelings of isolation as I stumbled through my teen years. And yet, I was gifted educational privilege.

Busia's poem reminds us that to escape violence, the enslaved fled to "a place of shelter" in the forest that was called Achimota. First a hiding place, it is now a wealthy neighborhood in greater Accra:

Sometimes it seems we are forgetting,
but so long as there are people alive who remember,
we will remember the meaning: (95)

Her poem reminds me of the loss my siblings would experience as they stayed away from Ghana for decades, the loss my nieces and nephews would experience for hardly having been there. Those of us who grew up in the diaspora have unwittingly had our connection to West Africa severed, in exchange for the better life our parents sought to provide. A shared belief that education will save us has now been passed down across several generations on both sides of my family. The grief embedded in that somewhat erroneous calculation is only revealed to me over time.

***

The story my white lesbian-feminist professor mother taught me had gaps in it. I was raised to be "colorblind." But I am not. One day my mother emailed me an article she came across about the damaging effects of colorblindness. "It tells what I did wrong," she wrote. I didn't open the article to read it. I'm certain it says the same things I tried to tell her years back, when our conversation about race resulted in her telling others that her daughter had called her a racist. In fear of moments like this, I had, like my white peers, been taught to avoid talking about race. I began my formal study of race when I went off to college, to study African American studies at a PWI (predominantly white institution). Not unlike my Ghanaian siblings who came to the United States for college, and who would also benefit from model minority myths built into the fabric of private-college financial schemas, I also wrestled with so many narratives of my identity forced upon me as I sought to pull together seemingly disparate pieces of myself.

Like the lesbians who birthed *Conditions*, and the editorial board that presided over issues with an "international focus," I too am inspired by Audre Lorde's journey in discovering all the pieces of herself. Her articulations have modeled for so many of us a path toward a better understanding of ourselves. While my words here may be worthy of the concern that Elly Bulkin expressed in her letter to Harriet Desmoines about the writings included in *Sinister Wisdom* as somewhat regrettably "inner-focused, abstract, sometimes, allegorical," decades later I find myself inspired by my encounter with *Conditions* precisely because it boldly made space for "lesbian imagination/consciousness" (6 August 1976). For it is always through the process of naming that I come to identify my own imbrication in the structures that shape how I experience the world.

As Beth Ritchie states in this issue: it is while doing activist work with other women in combatting gender-based violence that she is able to "feel whole as a woman, as a person or color, as an organizer and as a community activist" (183). The process of imagining, of coming into consciousness, is the necessary work of arriving at the intersection of all the pieces of one's self, in process and in relation to other women. Yet another intersection and intimacy I found in this issue were the interviews with Khayal and Utsa titled "There Are, Always, Have Been, Will Always Be Lesbians in India," articulations that affirmed what I have witnessed through my own extended family. I would not see in the ways that I do today if not for my habits of looking, honed through my efforts to identify where I fit in in the world, as I navigate communities in which not all of me is legible. I too learned to name myself as an act of survival.

My experience of my body signifying different things in different contexts has been a site of theorization for me since I was very young. I was able to blend in for the first time in my life while living in the Dominican Republic: I was not Black the way I was growing up in a pocket of white America, and I was not "white" the way I am seen in Ghana. Now, each return I make to Ghana, yes, there is forgetting—as Busia's poem reminds me—"But some remember still" (96). Looking down at where I stand with my brothers on the gravel driveway of our father's hotel in the Volta Region of Ghana, I see a small piece of myself in my little brother Kofi. Jutting out from his plastic flip-flop is the very same pinky toe that I have on both my feet. Round and stubby, tilted outward. A different color than mine, but the exact same toe.

Rachel Afi Quinn is an associate professor of Women's, Gender & Sexuality Studies and the Department of Comparative Cultural Studies at University of Houston. Her scholarship focuses on mixed race, gender, and sexuality in the African diaspora. Her first book, *Being La Dominicana: Race and Identity in the Visual Culture of Santo Domingo*, was published by University of Illinois Press in 2021. Her 2018 essay "Dominican Pride and Shame: Gender, Race and LGBT Activism in Santo Domingo" was published in *Small Axe: A Caribbean Journal of Criticism*. Rachel is passionate about mixed-media art and film and was a producer of the documentary *Cimarrón Spirit* (2015) about contemporary Afro-Dominican culture. She has recently initiated a series of digital humanities projects on race and visual culture. With her partner Eesha Pandit, she is a co-founding member of the transnational feminist collective leading South Asian Youth in Houston Unite (SAYHU), where she teaches about anti-Blackness, feminist theory, critical race theory, and identity in the global South.

CONDITIONS: FOURTEEN / INTERNATIONAL FOCUS II

— Response *by* Adriana M. Garriga-López

A Wormhole to the Black and Latina Lesbian Feminist World

Early on in the COVID pandemic of 2020, the Indian author Arundhati Roy wrote, "The pandemic is a portal."[2] Little did I know it would take me back in queer time to a pre-digital era when periodicals served as meeting grounds for writers to share stories, construct counterpublics, and feel each other across geographic space and social class. *Conditions: Fourteen / International Focus II*, published in 1987, reflects the global focus and liberatory impetus of the women's movement at the time, as well as the intensifying difficulties of sustaining work.

"We were barely able to publish this issue," note the editors in their introduction, marking the precariousness of their endeavor. Within its pages, however, is a trove of creative and intellectual power evidencing a joyful feminist community built on the critical investigation of women's lives, experiences, and desires across contexts. It harbors a deep reservoir of knowledge about different women's experiences. The issue opens with the portrait of a smiling elder Masai woman, a vision of Black female longevity and power. It offers autobiographical narratives about the strange loneliness of growing up Afro-German, features short stories partly told in Tagalog and Yiddish vernaculars (with accompanying glossaries for the reader), and contains the briefest glimpse of a Chinese woman nostalgic for Great Lakes she's never seen, as well as poems written in both English and Spanish.

---

2 Arundhati Roy, "The pandemic is a portal," *Financial Times*, April 3, 2020, https://www.ft.com/content/10d8f5e8-74eb-11ea-95fe-fcd274e920ca.

The web of short stories delivers us to an interstitial drawing of a writer at her desk, a typewriter in front and cats by her side, evidence of creativity and playful self-affirmation all around her. A writer's cave. A woman's desk. An intellectual dyke's lair. It might have made me a little nostalgic except that it still seems so relevant and thus not gone. Replace the typewriter with a computer, and a big part of the work is still just sitting at our keyboards surrounded by art and sending each other texts to confirm that what we are feeling and thinking is not wrong, that we are not crazy, that the world is indeed really this fucked up.

When Puerto Rican lesbian poet Luzma Umpierre asks Sandra María Esteves, "So you are still writing poetry?" Esteves responds, "I'll probably be writing poetry until the day I die" ("I Want What I Write to Be Necessary," 110). Because the writing and the living are pretty much the same thing. Esteves, of Puerto Rican and Dominican heritage, in turn demands of the late Julia de Burgos, "Why did you let the dragon slay you?" (118).

"Until the world comes around to a broader acceptance of a woman-centered orientation," asserts Kamili Anderson in her review of Jewelle Gomez's *Flamingoes and Bears*, our "vanguard poetry" leads the way through the bodies and dreams of women who refuse to fade. Breena Clarke, Cheryl Clarke's sister, reviews Anna Lee Walters's *The Sun Is Not Merciful*, stories of Native American women's courageous lives. Valerie Miner so enjoys Ann Oothuizen's (ed.) *Stepping Out*, a book of British women's short stories, she considers moving to London. And in the essays section, Margaret Nichols explains authoritatively "What Feminists Can Learn From the Lesbian Sex Radicals."

This retrospective look at *Conditions: Fourteen / International Focus II* opened a wormhole to the Black and Latina lesbian-feminist world that shaped me as a young queer and that set the stage for so much of what we think of as our contemporary movements for liberation. It reminded me that we have always lived and worked in the interstices, and that writing, reading, being read, and creating the conditions for others to write and read are but another method of loving and being loved.

Adriana María Garriga-López is an anthropologist and multidisciplinary artist. Born and raised in San Juan, Puerto Rico, Garriga-López is Associate Professor of Anthropology at Kalamazoo College in Michigan and Associate Faculty of the Brooklyn Institute for Social Research. She holds a PhD in anthropology (2010), as well as master of philosophy (2006) and master of arts (2003) degrees in anthropology from Columbia University in New York and a BA in cultural anthropology and comparative literature from Rutgers, the State University of New Jersey (2001), where she co-founded LLEGO! (The Queer People of Color Union). Visit her website at: www.adrianagarrigalopez. com.

CONDITIONS: FIFTEEN
— Response by Carmen Maria Machado

The Mourners

after Stuart Dybek

The boy next door said it sounded like they were grieving the dead over there, all that terrible moaning. He was right, in a way. They grieved in the living room, on the worn green couch; on the floor where the carpet concealed a trapdoor to the basement they didn't know existed. They grieved sitting up and lying down; in the pile of their own discarded dresses; even before the cold radiators they grieved. Against the countertops, in the bedroom. The bathtub, too, collected the messy puddles of their grieving. They did not grieve outside, though the animals that passed through the yard felt it, pulsing through the windows like the heat from a housefire. Sparrows, sorrow-struck and love-startled, abandoned their branches. Squirrels did not try for the birdseed. The grass grew wild.

They grieved because it'd been so long and so much had been unsaid. They grieved because no one had told them otherwise. They grieved because they'd known men and regretted it. They grieved because time had elapsed and time was elapsing. They grieved because the story of Rapunzel had been a terrible lie; in fact, the witch was her lover, and the tower the thing they'd built to keep them from the world. That story, and so many others, were lies, and for that their grief overflowed. Their grief tasted like ash but also the sea. It tasted like lemons and gasoline. It tasted like the knowledge we have from birth: that we must suck—mouth to the body of another—or we die.

There—in her house, though the other knew it as intimately as her own—they let their grief blossom, overflow. They grieved when they woke up and before they slept and throughout the longest days. They did other things—ate, drank, checked the mail—but mostly they grieved. Why do anything else when you can grieve for hours, days, years, stretched luxuriously beneath curtained windows and giclee prints and on quilts and someone else's knitting?

The grief kept them alive. Long after the boy next door was grown, married, widowered, buried, they were still grieving and as young as the day they'd began. No one else knew, though if they'd known, they would have not understood. They would have said, *They're sisters,* or, *they're roommates. They're the daughters of the widows who used to live there. I've heard about them. They're such good friends.* No would have understood the truth: They were warriors, on a warm battlefield, pushing back death.

Artist Statement

This piece, written for Sinister Wisdom *in commemoration of* Conditions: A Feminist Magazine of Writing for Women with an Emphasis on Writing by Lesbians, *contains references to the work of three writers who appear in issue fifteen (1988) of* Conditions: *Sapphire ("Eat"), Deborah Salazar ("They Were Sobbing . . ."), and Pamela Sneed ("Rapunzel").*

Carmen Maria Machado is the author of the bestselling memoir *In the Dream House* and the award-winning short story collection *Her Body and Other Parties*. She has been a finalist for the National Book Award and the winner of the Bard Fiction Prize, the Lambda Literary Award for Lesbian Fiction, the Lambda Literary Award for LGBTQ Nonfiction, the Brooklyn Public Library Literature Prize, the Shirley Jackson Award, and the National Book Critics Circle's John Leonard Prize. Her essays, fiction, and criticism have appeared in the *New Yorker*, the *New York Times*, *Granta*, *Vogue*, *This American Life*, *Harper's Bazaar*, *Tin House*, *McSweeney's Quarterly Concern*, *The Believer*, *Guernica*, *Best American Science Fiction & Fantasy*, *Best American Nonrequired Reading*, and elsewhere. She holds an MFA from the Iowa Writers' Workshop and has been awarded fellowships and residencies from the Guggenheim Foundation, Yaddo, Hedgebrook, and the Millay Colony for the Arts. She lives in Philadelphia and is the Abrams Artist-in-Residence at the University of Pennsylvania.

CONDITIONS: SIXTEEN
— Response by Red Washburn

Lesbian, Queer, and Trans Evolutions

After speaking to students about literary troublemaking, reading from her latest book *By My Precise Haircut*, and paying a tribute to Audre Lorde, Cheryl Clarke donated a box of books, including several issues of *Conditions*, to the Women's and Gender Studies Program at CUNY Kingsborough. After thirty years of *Conditions*, I started thinking about the importance of this publication again, one that highlighted the contributions of lesbians/queers of color and transgressions of gender across the spectrum. I am delighted to participate in *Sinister Wisdom*'s critical remembering of this publication. It is essential to archive and celebrate LGBTQ history and writing—not just as a reminder of the past, but rather to complicate time and space, reimagine it, and recast it as an ongoing social movement and genealogical knowledge project committed to the preservation of LGBTQ lives and voices. In particular, it behooves lesbians/queers now to lift up lesbian/queer life and cultural work at this political moment, post-Stonewall, when LGBTQ rights have been rolled back under a conservative government, even as we witness the promise of revolution with #MeToo and Black Lives Matter. The failure to do so might result in erasure, for no one will write about our lesbian/queer lives besides us—and if they do, might not do so accurately. In *Conditions: Sixteen / A Retrospective* (1989), many topics resurface that speak to the imminent danger that we are experiencing, including concerns with child custody, conversion therapy, colonialism/land, LGBTQ education, and sex work. These issues exist alongside the perils of assimilation, normativity, white supremacy, misogyny, and transphobia within our communities as well. Taken together, as I am reviewing *Conditions: Sixteen*, I am reflecting much on storytelling and living history then just as much as I am on survival and change now.

Conditions: Sixteen / A Retrospective could be classified as one of the greatest hits of lesbian/queer writing. It features innovative work—poetry, fiction, essays, and book reviews—by notable writers, such as Donna Allegra, Cheryl Clarke, Joy Harjo, Dorothy Allison, Gloria Anzaldúa, Audre Lorde, Samuel Ace (formerly Linda Smukler), Paula Gunn Allen, Elly Bulkin (interview with Blue Lunden, addressed as Doris Lunden), and Barbara Smith, among numerous others. Since then, several of the aforementioned writers have passed on, for example, Donna Allegra, Gloria Anzaldúa, Audre Lorde, Paula Gunn Allen, and Blue Lunden. Others have received prestigious awards, like Joy Harjo (Lifetime Achievement Award from the Native Writers' Circle of the Americas and the Wallace Stevens Award for mastery in the art of poetry from the Academy of American Poets, among others). Still others have received critical acclaim, like Gloria Anzaldúa, Cheryl Clarke, Audre Lorde, Barbara Smith, particularly from literary (LambdaLiterary.org), academic (National Women's Studies Association and the Audre Lorde Project), and Samuel Ace. These writers explore a plethora of themes: politics, language, genocide, racism, hunger, power, sexual abuse, spirituality, nature, land, intersectionality, and the literary canon.

While the entire issue is groundbreaking, I was especially interested in the writings of Barbara Smith, Audre Lorde, Pat Parker, and Cheryl Clarke, namely for their incisive analysis of the canon and politicization, power and difference, self-definition and intersectionality, and survival and social change. As a result of massive social movements, identities and bodies remain the focus of critical attention—for example, thinking about Black queer women's leadership and revisiting Kimberlé Williams Crenshaw's work on intersectionality during #MeToo. I remember reading Barbara Smith in grad school, and it is surreal to revisit her work now, post–Toni Morrison's passing and the fortieth anniversary of the Combahee River Collective Statement. Even now, in rereading "Toward a Black Feminist Criticism," I am struck by Smith's bold intervention into a straight white male canon and trailblazing of a Black feminist approach to literary criticism by repositioning Black women's voices as the foundation of the canon. She states, "A Black feminist approach to literature that embodies the realization that the politics of sex as well as the politics of race and class are crucially interlocking factors in the works of Black women writers is an absolute necessity" (9). It helps us move away from the ahistorical predilection to the focus on form without a political understanding of power and how the cultural domination of white men's literature exists at the exclusion of Black women's contributions. Likewise, I feel the political exigency of Audre Lorde's "Man-Child: A Black Lesbian Feminist's Response." This piece on Black survival, with a focus on Black male children makes more visible the demands currently being made by the Black Lives Matter movement, conceptualized and led by Black queer women Alicia Garza, Patrisse Cullors, and Opal Tometi. They are evident in this powerful passage: "For survival, black children in america must be raised to be warriors. For survival, they must also be raised to recognize the real enemy's many faces" (30). Her legacy knows no bounds. Similar to Smith and Lorde, Pat Parker's "Boots are being polished" picks up on the subjects of survival and resistance. I have done scholarly work on *Movement in Black*, but I still get chills rereading Pat Parker's work—not to mention hearing Cheryl Clarke herself read Pat Parker's work at the book launch of *The Complete Works of Pat Parker*, edited by *Sinister Wisdom*'s editor, Julie Enszer. Parker's poem is a chorus of revolution. In it, using repetition, the speaker offers a clarion call in the following lines:

They will not come
clothed in brown
and swastikas, or

bearing chests heavy   with
gleaming crosses.
The time and   need
for ruses are   over.
They will come
in business suits
to buy your homes
and bring bodies to
fill your jobs.
[. . .]
And they will come.
They will come for
the perverts

& it won't matter if you're
       homosexual, not a faggot
       lesbian, not a dyke
       gay, not queer
[. . .]
They will come for
the perverts
and where will
you be
When they come?[1]

This poem is very pertinent now. White supremacists are
in power, openly declaring their alliance to the KKK and white
terrorist organizations, same-sex marriage and reproductive rights
are at risk of being overturned by the Supreme Court governed by
Christian fundamentalism, trans people are banned the military,
and immigrant children are in detention facilities separated from

1 Pat Parker, The Complete Works of Pat Parker (New Haven: A Midsummer
Night's Press & Sinister Wisdom, 2016), 82–86.

their parents. In fact, it could have been written now. Parker's poem is still a call to action. It reminds us that an injury to one is an injury to all, that we must act in solidarity with marginalized people across differences and identities.

Cheryl Clarke, too, expounds on identity in "Committed Sex," using sex as a form of subversive distraction from the daily politics of white supremacist heteropatriarchal imperialism during the Reagan administration. She invokes the Edwin Meeses of then— and I think about Trump recently giving Meese the "Medal of Freedom," too. In "Committed Sex," the speaker says:

> i'll steal a vcr, make my own videos to be sexually aroused
> to get my mind off star wars and other wars
> [. . .]
> to get my mind off the cia, contras, and other wars
> in beirut, belfast, sharpeville, philly
> to sleep with my own kind naked under the stars
> to pose in a harness, to kiss her pussy (167)

The interminable wars, at home against Black people and of US international policy, resonate during this time as well, along with the direct mention of "quarantines," the former of which Cheryl Clarke and I—as co-editors, along with Morgan Gwenwald and Stevie Jones—also include as central themes in *Dump Trump: Legacies of Resistance* (*Sinister Wisdom* 110, Fall 2018). Overall, the pulse of Black lesbian-feminist writing is highlighted in this collection in ways that still hold up and encourage continued community-building.

I want to close this review by noting how some lesbian/queer feminist publications, perhaps even *Conditions* itself, might have evolved or for those still in circulation, might evolve now if they have not—the ways in which they should have further evaluated their evolution in relation to the realities of shifting identities in LGBTQ communities, namely trans and gender-nonconforming identities. Blue Lunden, interviewed by Elly Bulkin for "An Old Dyke's Tale" in this issue, is one such example. I recall the first time I learned of Blue Lunden at the Lesbian Herstory Archives, where her photograph towered over me in a tux and top hat, and I asked Deb Edel, one of the cofounders of the Lesbian Herstory Archives, about her. That was one of many conversations I had about butches, some of whom did not identify with the political category "woman." In diving into this interview, I learned more about Lunden than I had even after I visited Sugarloaf Women's Village, where I saw the film about her. I learned she was arrested in a bar. She fought with her father after it and then left her home because when she was . . . outed. Later, she got pregnant when she a sex worker, and shortly thereafter, she lost custody of her kid. She often struggled with substance abuse. She attended Gay Liberation Front dances and protests. More importantly, I learned she not only was gender-nonconforming, but also passed as a man. The latter was a revelation to me; moreover, throughout the interview, she discusses Christine Jorgensen, gender-affirming surgeries, and her own dysphoria quite candidly. She reveals the following:

> Later on I was falling in love with other girls and thinking of myself as a man trapped in a woman's body—I think I bought that kind of an idea for quite a long time. And when I did hit the bars, I had the right kind of build, I could pass as a boy and that was valued. It was considered really good that I had such small breasts, I didn't even have to wear a breastband. Women used to wrap their breasts, strap them down so that they wouldn't show. I didn't have to do that in order to pass. (69–70)

This story is significant and remains so in lesbian/queer feminist communities that are trans-inclusive.

Like Blue Lunden, Samuel Ace, now trans and genderqueer, addresses similar issues in his writing, most notably in his love letter to Linda Smukler called "Dear Linda" in *Meet Me There: Normal Sex & Home in three days. Don't wash* (2019). The continuum of butch and trans in lesbian/queer circles exists, and LGBTQ communities should respect self-definition and difference in this regard, rather than promoting misrepresentation, division, and exclusion that all lesbians/queers must share the same gender if gender-nonconforming. Our survival depends on it, especially now during this calamitous present. We have different social movements and different languages both then and now, but they are all historically linked and inextricably tied to fighting structural power and embracing the long struggle for freedom for LGBTQ folks. As Blue Lunden declared, "Telling stories about our experiences is our way of demonstrating that wisdom is *in* our community" (81). *Conditions: Sixteen / A Retrospective* provides a crucial angle of vision of how wisdom has traveled in lesbian/queer communities, a testament to the power of our words, and both a memory and a possibility of a better world for LGBTQ writers in which expression and representation are centered and honored. I am grateful for *Conditions*, as well as this celebration of it.

Red Washburn, PhD, is Associate Professor of English and Director of Women's and Gender Studies at CUNY Kingsborough. They also teach Women's and Gender Studies at Brooklyn College and the Graduate Center. They are the co-editor of *Women's Studies Quarterly*, published by the Feminist Press. Red's articles appear in *Journal for the Study of Radicalism*, *Women's Studies: An Interdisciplinary Journal*, and *Journal of Lesbian Studies*. Their essays are in several anthologies, including *Theory and Praxis: Women's and Gender Studies at Community Colleges*, *Introduction to Women's, Gender & Sexuality Studies: Interdisciplinary and Intersectional Approaches*, and *Trans Bodies, Trans Selves: A Resource for the Transgender Community*. They are the co-editor of Sinister Wisdom's *Dump Trump: Legacies of Resistance*, *45 Years: A Tribute to Lesbian Herstory Archive*, and *Trans/Feminisms*. Finishing

Line Press published their poetry collections *Crestview Tree Woman* and *Birch Philosopher X*. Their academic book *Irish Women's Prison Writing: Mother Ireland's Rebels, 1960-2010s* is forthcoming from Routledge. They received an ACLS/ Mellon fellowship for their next project *Nonbinary: Tr@ns-Forming Gender and Genre in Nonbin@ry Literature, Performance, and Visual Art*. Red is a coordinator at the Lesbian Herstory Archives as well as on the board of directors of Center for LGBTQ Studies (CLAGS) and *Sinister Wisdom*.

CONDITIONS: SEVENTEEN
— Response by Naomi Extra

Tending to Our Struggles for Freedom

In a letter to *Conditions* editor Cheryl Clarke, an unnamed reader described the aftermath of the Montreal massacre of 1989: "We all lived on the edge of rage and tears here." The letter described the targeted attack on women at UNV by Marc Lépine, a disgruntled man who was angry that women were taking jobs that he felt men were entitled to. Although *Conditions: Seventeen* was published thirty years ago, many of the themes and concerns in the issue—violence against women, flagrant attacks on the rights of queer folks, and the concerted effort to squash freedom of expression by seeking to eliminate arts funding—resonate in today's political landscape. In the issue, the editors describe "the attacks by Jesse Helms and the American Family Association on NEA-funded artists," particularly lesbian writers. An article written by Diane Palladino entitled "HIV Infection: The Construction of the Disease in Women" points to women's bodies as yet another site of HIV infection. According to Palladino, women were "invisible recipients of the disease" while also being framed as "responsible recipients of the disease" and existed without adequate services. The issue coheres around a set of themes—intimacy, touch, care, safety, and community—that inform larger conversations around lesbian freedom and expression.

In "Our Gift of Touch," Joan Nestle reminds readers that lesbian touch is not to be taken for granted. She asks, "How in such a world as this, where guns and government crush tenderness every day, can you find your way to that woman's small hidden place?" By extension, in "Bitches Bite," a story by Cherry Muhanji, we see that lesbian communal spaces are not to be taken for granted either.

In the story, "Wintergreen" is a fictional club that hosts themed nights like "Bitches Bite" where women compete for the best male celebrity look. Wintergreen's is a "place where some women, unable to tell the lyin' motha fuckahs they lived with or the women they didn't, how being who they couldn't be most of the time felt good." The story portrays the dimensions of lesbian liberation that are not only about access to space but the rich communities that emerge in these spaces.

In "Excerpts from *Dyketionary*" by Joni Van Dyke, we see how language can function as a key site of queer liberation. Van Dyke challenges "heterocentricity" in language and discourse by using her handwriting as opposed to standard typeface in the excerpt. "The motivation for this dyketionary comes from the awareness that one of the boys' strategies in keeping womyn apart and oppressed is their control of language," she writes. The dyketionary contains words like "faghag," "herstory," and "lesbian," along with translations of each word into Japanese. This pivot away from Anglocentricity is present throughout the issue.

In "Yuriko, Da Svidanya," Hitomi Sawabe writes on the Japanese proletarian writer Yuriko Miyamoto and her lesbian romance with Russian literature specialist and translator Yoshiko Yuasa. Sawabe recovers this history and asks the reader to consider how the couple might have fared had they not lived under the crushing pressure of compulsory heterosexuality. Sawabe writes: "What if they had been able to believe more in the meaning of their love and their life? What if they had lived a half-century later, when feminism had won rights for women? What if their sexual relationship had been more successful? My 'what-if's' know no limit."

Conditions: Seventeen also contains a cluster of erotic poems. Short poems like "Orange Poem" by Anne Haines offer feminist pleasure portrayed in short bursts of metaphoric language:

I feel sweet light
about to burst

from me, at the smallest
pressure
a cool globe
exploding
on your tongue.

"Packing," by Carolyn Gammon, captures the butch joy and pleasure. The poem's title is a cheeky double entendre that speaks to both packing for travel and packing one's genitals. Pat Califia's poem "I Love Butches" is a celebration of butch aesthetics: "The muscles, the short hair, / The refusal to pick up / Where their mothers left off."

As the US continues to grapple with the COVID-19 pandemic, the short story "2280" by Mariana Romo-Carmona projects into a future that resonates to the present with chilling accuracy. In "2280," Romo-Carmona presents a world in which fiction is difficult to discern from reality. "There is no way of knowing what is fact, fiction, reenactments, documentary broadcasts, hologram transmissions, simulated news events—human history is complete chaos." One can only think of the more recent crisis of "fake news" and "alternative facts." "2280" also makes reference to environmental disaster, a "Great Infection" that has caused mass disease, the persecution of "brown-skinned human beings" (who are also blamed for the transmission of disease), and a government that has "turned against its own people." It's nearly impossible to read "2280" and not think of 2020—a year of social uprising, political instability, and a global pandemic.

In reading *Conditions: Seventeen*, it's also hard not to think about the vicious attacks on women's sexual freedom in more recent years. In 2018 we saw the swearing in of Brett Kavanaugh onto the US Supreme Court despite strong evidence of prior sexual misconduct/assault. We have also witnessed the continued attempts to overturn *Roe v. Wade* instigated by Donald Trump and his cronies. The rights of those who identify as trans, disabled,

LGBTQ, immigrant, and women have been under near-constant attack. It is within this context that *Conditions: Seventeen* demands to be read and reread with a great sense of attention and urgency. The issue reminds us that social progress does not follow a linear course. Freedoms aren't permanent, nor do they come overnight. Therefore we must tend to our freedom struggles with diligence, joy, and affirmation.

WANTED: ARTWORK FOR MAGAZINE COVER

Conditions, a nationally distributed magazine of writing by women with an emphasis on writing by lesbians, is interested in receiving submissions for its cover. The editors have no specific preconception as to subject matter or theme, and will consider any form appropriate for an 8½"x5" black and white cover bearing the title of the magazine and the issue number at the top. This might be a line drawing or other graphic, a photograph, or a half-tone of a painting, a collage, or sculpture.

The circulation of Conditions is currently 2,500 and is expected to increase in the next year. Artists whose work was used on the covers of the first four issues are Irene Peslikis, Joyce Kozloff, Harmony Hammond, and Betsy Damon. Payment to contributors is two copies of Conditions.

Please send a photocopy and not the original work to Conditions, P.O. Box 56, Van Brunt Station, Brooklyn, New York 11215. Only photocopies sent with a stamped self-addressed envelope will be returned.

p.o. box 56, van brunt station, brooklyn, n.y. 11215

conditions

CARROLL OLIVER, REMEMBRANCES

Photograph by Kelsey Lindsey

Carroll Oliver

'LIKE A BIRD THAT FLEW / TANGLED UP IN BLUE': NOTES FOR CARROLL

Akasha Hull

Carroll Phyllis Oliver was passionate in everything she did—which pushed her into extremes. A perfectionist who wanted to make her Marxist analyses pristine, her writing impeccable, her activism effective, she often lapsed into inaction when her efforts did not reach her impossible goals.

She was beautiful—precocious in looks, intellect, sophistication. She told me a story about flight attendants (we called them stewards and stewardesses in those days) who served her drinks when she was twelve years old.

We were friends, lovers, comrades, colleagues—drawn together by attraction of body and mind. Soul sisters. We once had a midnight-to-dawn telephone conversation, complete with journal sharing and sky-gazing silences. Another highlight was a vacation at a campground in Puerto Rico (she luxuriated in water/ the sea).

During my visits to her, we rode miles of New York City subways, walked many long crosstown blocks. She loved Bob Dylan's "Tangled Up in Blue."

Unfortunately for Carroll, addiction was too easy, life too complicated. As she lay dying of AIDS in a City hospital, I couldn't make the trip from California to New York to see her. My dear friend, Martha Zingo, went up from Delaware and said goodbye for me.

Akasha Hull, PhD, is a literary activist and professor emeritus at the University of California, Santa Cruz (www.akashahull.com). She has written poetry, short stories, articles, reviews, a novel

(*NEICY*, 2012), and other works that explore the personal-political-spiritual dimensions of Black women's lives. These include *But Some of Us Are Brave* (co-edited); *Color, Sex, and Poetry: Three Women Writers of the Harlem Renaissance*; *Healing Heart: Poems*; and *Soul Talk: The New Spirituality of African American Women*. Based in Little Rock, Arkansas, she spends rewarding time writing, connecting with people, and organizing her papers and photographs. Her most recent publication is a suite of COVID-era poems in *This Is How We Come Back Stronger* (And Other Stories, 2021).

Snapshot courtesy of Elly Bulkin

Dorothy Allison in the foreground and Carroll Oliver seated

RAZOR-SHARP CRITICAL INTELLIGENCE
Cheryl Clarke

Carroll was kind, brilliant, and a style setter.
—Kevin Sampson, cousin,
from correspondence with co-editors (2020)

Carroll Oliver was a member of the *Conditions* editorial collective from 1981 to 1983. I met her first in the late 1970s at one of the first two Black Feminist Retreats organized by Barbara Smith, Demita Frazier, Beverly Smith, and others in the Black lesbian and feminist community of Boston. As was my wont at that time, I pushed Carroll—who was about nineteen years old—about her sexual identity. "Are you a lesbian?" She looked at me shyly and said, "I don't know yet," waving her hand up and down as if to say, "Don't pin me down yet. Go away." I thought, *How brave and honest.* But I didn't admit of any mutability of identity/ies then, which young queer folk were just beginning to enunciate, demand, and practice, in fact.

Brooklyn was the site of our second encounter, at the first *Conditions* collective meeting of the new members/editors and the three founding editors/members: Elly Bulkin, Jan Clausen, and Rima Shore. The fourth founding editor, Irena Klepfisz, had resigned shortly after *Issue Seven.* New members Dorothy Allison, Jewelle Gomez, Mirtha Quintanales, and Carroll greeted me as I entered Elly's apartment in Park Slope, late. I remember, from then on, Carroll's face—with sometimes a wry and at other times a laughing expression of *I know what's going on here*—at many of the subsequent meetings we held in Manhattan and Brooklyn. One meeting, I remember, Carroll held at her family's apartment on 108th Street in Manhattan. I remember she took full charge of hosting the meeting and was confident and proud of her leadership. I remember catching a glimpse of her mother, Vernell Oliver, coming in from her Saturday errands, smiling briefly at us meeting in the living room, and then disappearing into one of a number of rooms along the narrow hallway of this splendid Upper West Side apartment. The physical resemblance between Carroll and Vernell was quite striking in every way—i.e., tall height, slenderness, facial features—except complexion. Carroll's mother was a dark brown and Carroll a tan red.

Jan Clausen (1976–82), Conditions founding editor, says this:

> I remember Carroll's razor-sharp critical intelligence, and how I—at the advanced age of 32!—looked forward to the impact of her youthful energy and fresh generational perspective on the work of the Conditions collective. (Remembrance, 9/7/20)

Clearly, Carroll was smart, reliable, responsible, and patient with the elders—the rest of us. Barbara Smith and the late Gloria Joseph were two of her mentors, both of whom knew Carroll at Hampshire College in Amherst, Massachusetts, from which she graduated in 1975. Her anti-establishment politics were deeply rooted. Gloria Joseph said this of Carroll in the "Acknowledgements" section of Common Differences: Conflicts in Black and White Feminist Perspectives, which she co-authored with Jill Lewis: "I would like to mention Carroll Oliver, who was my student assistant [at Hampshire College] and an outstanding worker" (1986).

The last time I saw Carroll was at the MLA Conference in DC in 1986, thirty-four years ago. She and Akasha (Gloria) Hull, Black feminist scholar, had come together. We greeted each other briefly at the end of the panel. Carroll was pregnant. Of course, as always with myself, when it is too late, I wish I had been more extensive. I can't remember, at this writing, from whom I learned Carroll had died. She was thirty-five years old. Jan Clausen continues with her reflection of Carroll:

The overlap of [my and Carroll's] editorial roles was extremely brief, but I came away impressed with the seriousness of [Carroll's] commitment to a blend of activism and intellectual work. I also caught glimpses of a tart sense of humor and a healthy intolerance for bullshit hiding inside the reserved demeanor she brought to those initial meetings. I wish I knew how the rest of us looked to Carroll!

Conditions was reputed for its archly critical book reviews, exquisite poetry, excellent fiction, and exhilarating essays. Angering some. Engaging many. (One Black lesbian academic living in LA confided to me, in 1984 that *Conditions: Nine* was the best news she'd received since she'd moved to LA in 1982, which she said she wanted to leave after her first week.) Carroll wrote two book reviews for *Conditions*—which is yeowoman's work then and now. Writing book reviews for the magazine was expected of editors. So, Carroll yeowoman-ed up twice in the two years she was an editor: writing reviews of J. R. Roberts' *Black Lesbians: An Annotated Bibliography* (*Conditions: Eight*, 1982) and of Judith Schwarz's *Radical Feminists of Heterodoxy* (*Conditions: Nine*, 1983). She was acerbic, naïve, well-educated (and not just from college), a kind of wistfulness about her, and hopeful.

I will close by recalling Carroll's reviews. Both of the works under review were edited/authored by two white feminists: J. R. Roberts and Judith Schwarz. Carroll's reviews were evaluative, respectful, and celebratory.

Carroll hurriedly gives Roberts's bibliography credit as "a terribly necessary work." By the time she joined *Conditions*, Carroll included herself within the community of lesbians, as she goes on to caution that "white women examining and documenting *our* [lesbian] lives and struggles have not yet been appropriately addressed." Carroll critiques Roberts's "selective indexing," i.e., eliding or erasing key issues of identity, of *Azalea: A Magazine By and For Third World Lesbians* and *Conditions: Five / The Black*

Women's Issue. Both publications' editorial control, says Carroll Oliver, was in the "hands of Black—or other Third World—Lesbians," amplifying an under-acknowledged cultural contribution of Black lesbian-feminists to the Women in Print Movement of the 1970s and '80s.

At a collective meeting, Carroll says, "I'm finding myself really interested in Grace Nail Johnson." Was Grace Nail Johnson,[1] the wife of James Weldon Johnson and the only Black woman member of the West Village women's group Heterodoxy, into the woman-and-woman bent of its devotees? During our meeting that day, Carroll and Elly got into an intense and critical discussion of *Heterodoxy* and the rich issues it raises. Carroll offers an illuminating disquisition of Grace Nail Johnson's influence on Black modernism, and says this of the shortcomings of Schwarz's *Heterodoxy*:

> *Heterodoxy* offers surprisingly little information about Grace Nail Johnson's life. Who was she? What did she do

---

1 Johnson was the light-skinned, patrician wife of Harlem Renaissance writer and arbiter James Weldon Johnson (1876–1938) and remained a force in sustaining her husband's legacy and championing African American culture, organizations, and people. Grace Nail Johnson, fifteen years younger than James Weldon Johnson, was married for twenty-eight years until she and James Weldon were involved in a car accident on Cape Cod. James Weldon was killed and Grace lingered in a coma for two weeks. When she awoke from her coma, James Weldon was dead. Grace Nail died at ninety-one in New York in 1976. She spent the rest of her life after 1938 with Ollie Jewel Sims Okala, whom the Johnsons had met as a nurse before James Weldon's death. Okala was Grace Nail Johnson's executor. Okala died in 2001 in the same apartment she and Grace Nail had lived in for nearly forty years. As a testament to their relationship, Okala's ashes were buried in the Nail family plot with those of the two Johnsons and the rest of the Nail family. Grace Nail Johnson contributed James Weldon Johnson's papers and her own to Yale University, creating the James Weldon Johnson and Grace Nail Johnson Papers housed in the Beinecke Rare Books Collection at Yale University. Grace Nail Johnson also contributed her own papers, and offered other Black writers the opportunity to contribute their papers to the collection. There has been no real or sustained research on either Johnson (nothing on Grace), though both were movers and shakers (doubly and singly) in New York City (Black) culture and politics for half a century. They both loved to party (Co-Editors' Note).

[What she did is well-documented.]? What was she like? What were her concerns? Again Schwarz offers few clues. Has Grace Nail Johnson been lost? It seems difficult to believe there is no other information about her, if only in her capacity as Mrs. James Weldon Johnson. . . . I was confused by Schwarz's failure to discuss what it meant for Grace to be Heterodoxy's only black member. Why was she the only Black woman ever to join the [Heterodoxy]. . . . To what extent was Grace's light skin an issue in all this?

These questions renew my desire to take up the study of Grace Nail Johnson, who has enchanted me for at least forty years.

Carroll Phyllis Oliver was born in Elizabeth, New Jersey, June 4, 1957, and died, June 23, 1992, of AIDS at Terence Cardinal Cooke Hospital "on a ward of minority women who were dying of [AIDS] . . . when we didn't know much about the disease," according to Kevin Sampson, her close cousin. Sampson, a wood sculptor who builds memorials and altars, created his first altar for Carroll, his "favorite cousin." (Sampson has also made altars for friends who died of AIDS during the early 1990s— https://folkart.org/mag/ kevin-sampson.) Also, according to Sampson, Carroll became involved in Santeria[2] "in hopes of a cure." After Carroll's death, her mother, Vernell McCarroll Oliver (1922–2012), gave Sampson the items from Carroll's altars. And from these he constructed an altar. He says this of his bond with Carroll:

I carved a figure of her and used her Santeria objects in the altar. I created a boat with her sitting in it, to help ease her journey into the next life. . . . My intention was not just to create a memorial, but to be involved in her transition to

---

2   Santeria is a syncretic African and Caribbean faith, dating back to the beginning of the trans-Atlantic slave trade, whose religious-cultural center is said to be Cuba still. Santeria fuses Yoruban (West African) and Euro-Catholic beliefs and practices. Santeria is still observed throughout the Black world.

the afterlife . . . I knew that even death couldn't separate us forever. That piece I did formed a bond with her death, looking at it . . . as a natural transition. . . . We grew up like siblings. I still mourn her. (Correspondence with *SW* co-editors, 2020)

I mourn Carroll anew.

SNAPSHOT LESBIAN LOVE CELEBRATION

This snapshot celebrates and honors Yeva Johnson and the single lesbian.

I've wanted to open up submissions to include individuals celebrating their lesbian loves and when I queried Yeva Johnson and she said she was single, but could do something around the unrequited loves she celebrated and honored, I thought: Yes! I said I would love to see what she comes up with. Not too long afterwards, I received these pieces within a bigger framework.

These four poems are from a larger body of work: *A Queer Bouquet of Lesbian Love* which includes 13 poems. I picked four, but I love them all. I am thrilled to include Yeva Johnson's work which I see as being among the finest meteorite flares in our sky, celebrating our time. —Roberta Arnold

Boom Boom
With Gratitude to Tomas Moniz & the BIPOC Writing Community

Heartbeat, every dream
I never let extinguish.
Ventricular sac – my family.
From carotid blood flow
to mitral valve, that crush
on the cute librarian still beats
under the Aortic Arch.
The right atrium is where I wear
my rose-colored glasses
and there are bits of my sleeve
plastered all over the pericardium.
Despite a septum, there's a softness
to the whole enterprise.

Electrical impulses keep that tricuspid
valve flapping, even with the small
plaques that softly push me
toward the cliff of death.
From the superior vena cava
all the way to the apex,
I always feel the love,
the love, the love, the love.

Water Play

I know   when we are together   we flit and splash   all is soft

smiles   in the shallows   interior laughter

                              The waterfall of my

self   drowns you   Great gulps of water

splash   across your face   up your nose

At first refreshing   perhaps   but then the thunder of me

never stops   and it's too much
too much
       too too much You can't breathe   or even   open your eyes

Water   on the lungs   burns
burns like fire

Wait!   you say   Let me come up for air

       But there is no air   only   me   showering

raining   splattering   pounding   shattering

on the rocks at your feet

~   ~   ~   ~   ~   ~   ~

~   ~   ~   ~   ~   ~   ~

What   you don't know

is   when you   toss me   out   I scramble

to survive   the vacuum   world   of your

disregard   I flop helplessly in that   arid

desert wash   My gills   open and close

and open   sigh   and close   But it's no use

I am seared   inside   and out   by the cleavage

You are   already departed   You never see me

gasping   without the sea   of your gaze   I yearn

to undulate   to love   to swim

All   I can do is   croak   in that   whisper

only fish have -   your name   -   and so invoke

a tremendous   cascade of   mountain waters

to swirl   us toward   the eddies   once more   together

For the Womxn whom I have yet to meet, apologies to those I've mistaken for her

With gratitude to Caroline M. Mar & the BIPOC Writing Community

I gave you some of my favorite books of all time: J. California Cooper's *Family*, James Baldwin's *Another Country*, Gloria Naylor's *Mama Day*, Maria Dermoût's *The Ten Thousand Things*, Toni Morrison's *Song of Solomon*, & Audre Lorde's *Zami: A New Spelling of My Name*.
I didn't even know if you liked to read.

I shared my belief that at least one person in the universe
could understand me, accept me and love me all at the same time
when I confessed my hope that it might be you.
You looked at me with pity, "honored" by my openness, but said
sorry it wasn't you.

I gave you my phone number. I thought I was unique until I met
myriad other women who had done the same for the hottest
barrista in Berkeley. And then I felt shame – I didn't mean to
objectify you.

I gave you the most heartfelt crush letters, every last one
of them on UNICEF stationary, each stamp applied with love.
Did you recycle them, I wonder?

I gave you thirty minutes to tell me any hidden secret or shame
because you trusted I would never divulge and would always
accept you. You never knew that those minutes could have been
renewed for life.

I played you a song I composed just for you and gifted
every poem with my heart's secret longing tucked inside to you.
My melodies and verse passed through you, nothing to grasp, to
hold fast.

Now I take back the love I've showered indiscriminately on so many fleeting infatuations as I develop the wisdom to recognize the potential for real love and the courage to return your touch when you reach out. No more missing ships.

Fruits of the Sapphic Tree of Love
With love for Devi Peacock, Ellen Bass, Janet Brown, & Lindsey Wild

> Perhaps for a lesbian like me
> sustained romantic
> love is not in the cards
> no matter how I might yearn.
> Even so, I know
> that Sappho has much
> to offer, so many delicious
> varieties of passionate affection
> among and between womxn,
> friendship, that bond among
> poets writers and artists,
> that ardor between poets
> writers artists and their
> admirers, the community
> of womxn loving womxn
> in myriad ways.
> Queer love brings joy, delights,
> whether solo or in combination,
> so I slake my thirst for connection
> at the well of gratitude
> nestled at the base
> of the Sapphic Tree of Love.

IN TRIBUTE TO KAY TOBIN LAHUSEN, GAY ACTIVIST AND DOCUMENTARIAN (1930-2021)

Marcia M. Gallo

From my files, @2002:

Hello Marcia Gallo,
At long last, a get-together in Wilmington! Our schedule is clear March 21 and 22, and we would be pleased to see you on either day or both days. If you can spare us only one day, okay, although we have enough stuff to show you for two afternoons if you can manage it. (Barbara is not a morning person.) We have papers, photos, etc. to share with you.
Congratulations on your choice of the history of DOB as a Ph.D. project!
Call us to discuss details. We could buy you a lunch on the day you come.
In gay spirits,
Kay Tobin Lahusen (and Barbara Gittings)

P.S. We still have photos of your visit years ago with Del and Phyl when we lived in Barbara's mother's house in Wilmington, a house long since sold. We're condo dwellers now.

Wilmington, DE; 1995:
L-R: (back) Carmen Vázquez, Barbara Gittings, Del Martin
(front) Marcia Gallo, Kay Tobin Lahusen

As a lesbian historian of social justice movements, I have been blessed over the last two decades with opportunities to meet and talk with remarkable women who created the homophile and gay liberation movements, sometimes developing long-lasting friendships in the process. Kay Tobin Lahusen is one whose friendship I treasure most. Her generosity – which is apparent even in an early e-mail communication she sent me about a delayed in-person meeting - was only surpassed by her depth of knowledge and commitment to LGBTQ+ people and our equality, which never wavered for fifty years. Kay deserves to be much better acknowledged for her enormous contributions to LGBTQ history. Too often overshadowed by her more famous sisters in the movements, she insured that their efforts were made visible. Through her prodigious body of work, especially her documentary photographs and written archives, she has left us a treasure trove of homophile and gay liberation images and stories.

Born January 5, 1930 and raised in Cincinnati, Ohio by her grandparents, Kay Lahusen came to terms with her love for another young woman as a teenager. "I decided that I was right and the world was wrong and that there couldn't be anything wrong with this kind of love," she told me. Kay moved to Boston after a devastating break-up to work as a researcher for the *Christian Science Monitor*, where, she noted, "they filed homosexuality under 'Vice'." In 1961, she contacted New York psychiatrist Richard Robertiello after reading his book *Voyage to Lesbos: The Psychoanalysis of a Female Homosexual*. As she remembered years later, "I didn't want to be cured...I wanted to find out how to meet other lesbians." Robertiello told her about DOB, she wrote to them, and the person who answered Kay's letter was New York chapter organizer Barbara Gittings. They soon met in person at a DOB picnic. Kay began attending meetings, planning programs, and helping with the chapter's newsletter. When she started publishing in the DOB magazine The *Ladder* in 1963, she picked "Tobin" out of the phonebook to use as her "DOB name." According to her, "Lahusen is too hard to pronounce!" Her early activism led both to a lifelong relationship with Gittings (1931-2007) and an ongoing commitment to organizing and documenting LGBTQ movements.

The visionary leadership she shared with Barbara helped propel DOB forward in the 1960s through a variety of means. Among them were the monumental changes they made to the group's most important organizing tool, The *Ladder*. After Gittings became editor in 1962, she insisted to DOB's leaders that it was imperative to change the "face" of public representations of lesbianism through the use of Lahusen's photographic portraits of DOB friends, allies, and *Ladder* readers on the magazine's covers. It was a ground-breaking decision. Readers agreed wholeheartedly; Kay's portraits helped expand the magazine's viability, visibility, and popularity. Barbara also added the words "A Lesbian Review" to The *Ladder* cover in 1964, in bold typeface, marking the first time the word "lesbian" was used as part of an ongoing magazine title. Together, they greatly expanded the magazine's content as well, soliciting or reprinting articles from well-known authors as well as presenting both sides of debates over the movement's changing attitudes toward research and activism. Aided by regular financial contributions from an anonymous wealthy closeted lesbian, The *Ladder* became a well-regarded monthly magazine that was distributed through a national network of "alternative" or academic bookstores as well as mailed to a growing list of subscribers, albeit still in envelopes with no return address in a continuing effort to guard against unwanted disclosure.

Kay and Barbara also pushed for increased collaborations with activists in the mostly male homophile groups - including the Mattachine Society of Washington, DC, led by Franklin Kameny — to build the larger homophile movement. Soon they would join Kameny and other gay and lesbian advocates in adapting tactics of the Black civil rights movement, organizing homophile pickets at public buildings such as the pre-Stonewall (1965-1969) "Annual

Reminder" days held on July 4 at Independence Mall in Philadelphia. Kay was always there with her camera to document these historic pickets, as well as those in other cities such as New York and Washington, DC, making her one of the earliest photographers of the homophile groups as they began to evolve into the gay liberation movement.

L: Photo of Eckstein picketing in 1966 by Kay Tobin Lahusen; R: photo of Lahusen picketing in 1969 by Nancy L. Tucker

In the mid-60s, she and Barbara continued to work within the New York chapter of DOB, where they promoted new leadership and ideas, including the then-radical views of DOB activists such as Ernestine "Eckstein" (a pseudonym), a young Black woman from Indiana with college experience in the civil rights movement. Ernestine had moved to New York in the early 1960s and joined DOB. She quickly became Vice President of the local chapter. Kay's 1966 portrait of her, taken in Washington Square Park, appeared on the cover of The *Ladder* in June of that year – the first Black lesbian to be featured on the cover of a national gay magazine. Kay and Barbara also conducted a wide-ranging, five-hour interview with Eckstein and included an edited version of it in the same issue. Eckstein thoughtfully and carefully distinguished between the Black and gay rights movements. She urged homophiles to increase their public activism as well as continue their educational work with other civil rights groups and the public. She also joined the pickets at federal buildings in Washington, D.C., one of very few women and the only Black person to be photographed doing so. Although Eckstein left DOB and New York for the San Francisco Bay area in the late 1960s, her ideas about activism helped shape DOB's program into the 1970s.

By the late 1960s, Lahusen was devoting her considerable energies not only to changing public representations of lesbians and gay men but also to ensuring that their stories would be recorded. In 1969, she stepped from behind the camera to join the Annual Reminder picket line herself, just days after the Stonewall riot took place in New York. Her dedication to the new gay liberation movement that followed in the wake of Stonewall continued to grow: she was a founding member of the Gay Activists Alliance (GAA) as well as Gay Women's Alternative (GWA). Perhaps most importantly, with her seemingly ever-present camera, she documented protests, picnics, and the hundreds, then thousands, of people who were mobilizing in New York and Philadelphia for gay liberation in the early 1970s. Her portraits range from well-known activists such as Craig Rodwell, Sylvia Rivera and Marsha P. Thompson to ordinary lesbian and gay male couples, which made visible wide-ranging LGBTQ peoples. These years also saw the publication of *The Gay Crusaders*, the groundbreaking collection of first-person activist accounts that Kay authored, with fellow activist Randy Wicker included as co-author due to the publisher's insistence on gender parity. She conducted and transcribed audio interviews and included her photographic portraits of fifteen GAA activists in one of the earliest books to document the life experiences of some of the leaders of the new movement.

Her commitments extended to challenging the homophobic policies of national institutions such as the American Library

Association (ALA) and the American Psychiatric Association (APA) with Gittings, Kameny, and other activists in the early 1970s. At the ALA convention in Dallas, Texas in 1971, Gittings helped create and staffed the outrageous "Hug A Homosexual" booth, designed both to shock and raise awareness. As was typically Barbara, she not only happily hugged other homosexuals but was photographed – by Lahusen and others - enthusiastically kissing author Isabel Miller on the lips while the librarians looked on in amazement. She capitalized on the shock value by working with other ALA members for the next decade on the Gay Task Force she helped create.

She and Kay also helped to change the longstanding association of homosexuality with disease. When Gittings convinced gay "Doctor H. Anonymous" (John Fryer) to speak to his colleagues at their annual convention in 1972, Lahusen photographed him wearing his disguise, an image that went viral. This historic encounter with one of their own members was one that the psychiatrists in the audience could not ignore. The next year, in 1973, the APA removed homosexuality from its list of mental disorders, a huge leap forward for LGBTQ equality. After years of damning diagnoses and destructive remedies, as Barbara commented to me in 2003, "all of a sudden, we were cured!"

Throughout the next twenty years, they continued their activism locally - in Philadelphia, New York, and Wilmington, Delaware - as well as nationally. In the 2000s, during Barbara's increasingly serious health challenges, their movement work extended to ensuring that their papers, photographs, videos, books, magazines, buttons, tee shirts and other paraphernalia would be securely archived and made available to the public via the New York Public Library. I spent a few Saturdays at their home office in Wilmington in 2006, working with LGBTQ television historian Steven Capsuto, who was helping them collate their collection for NYPL. It was a personal and political milestone for Kay when, in 2017 and 2018, Jason Baumann, NYPL Associate Director and

Coordinator of Humanities and LGBT Collections, worked with her to create the 50th anniversary exhibit and publication *Love and Resistance: Stonewall 50* (W.W. Norton, 2019), which showcases her decades of gay movement photography along with the iconic images of sister activist photographer Diana Davies.

After Gittings' death in 2007, Kay continued to be a dedicated advocate. From their new home in Kennett Square, PA, where she and Barbara had organized a "gay lunch table" at their independent living community immediately after moving in, she loved nothing more than to continue to share her memories and experiences of the movement to which she had dedicated her life. And she never stopped being passionate about LGBTQ visibility: at our last in-person meeting in January 2020, we discussed the upcoming Democratic Presidential primary. I asked her who she was supporting. "Why, Pete Buttigieg, of course!" (We agreed to disagree.)

It also is so typical of her that, up until just a few weeks before her death on May 26, 2021, at age 91, Kay welcomed phone calls and short interviews with activists, students, and researchers. I know this because I sent many of them to her, always checking first to make sure it was ok. "Oh, sure, Marcia…just make sure they don't call during lunch…and not too late at night either." Her passion for "her people" – all LGBTQ people – never ceased. My deep appreciation for her, personally and politically, never will, either.

For further information:

Kay Tobin and Randy Wicker, *The Gay Crusaders* (Paperback Library, 1972)

Marcia M. Gallo, *Different Daughters: A History of the Daughters of Bilitis and the Rise of the Lesbian Rights Movement* (Carroll & Graf, 2006; Seal Press, 2007)

Eric Marcus, *Making Gay History* (HarperCollins, 2002) Also: numerous episodes on makinggayhistory.com: see especially Stonewall 50 Minisode https://makinggayhistory.com/podcast/stonewall-50-minisode-3-barbara-gittings-kay-lahusen/ and Remembering Kay Lahusen https://makinggayhistory.com/podcast/remembering-kay-lahusen/

New York Public Library, Barbara Gittings and Kay Tobin Lahusen Gay History Papers and Photographs http://archives.nypl.org/mss/6397

William Way LGBT Community Center, Philadelphia PA; Barbara Gittings and Kay Tobin Lahusen Collection, 1950-2009 https://static1.squarespace.com/static/5bdf5ea9266c07394b298351/t/5d2f3e42063a5c00019b2a2d/1563377218582/MsColl03.pdf

Tracy Baim and Kay Lahusen, *Barbara Gittings: Gay Pioneer* (Prairie Avenue Productions, 2015)

BOOK REVIEW

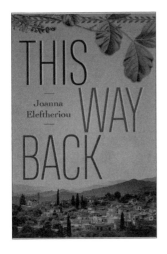

This Way Back
By **Joanna Eleftheriou**
West Virginia University Press 2020
Paperback, $23.99

Reviewed by Barrie Jean Borich

The Corners of Her Beauty: a review of Joanna Eleftheriou's
This Way Back.

What is lesbian identity and where can we find it on a map? We might be tempted to say the Greek Isle of Lesbos, but even this mythic home of the poet Sappho (in other than pandemic times still a popular lesbian tourist destination) is 500 miles from the island center of Joanna Eleftheriou's 2020 memoir-in-essays, *This Way Back,* a book about her deep familial identity with another small place in the Mediterranean, the Greek/Turkish Island of Cyprus.

Cyprus is a geography with a green line across its center—on one side Greek and on the other side Turkish, not unlike the line Eleftheriou describes as dividing herself in the years before she proclaimed her lesbian identity. Part American, part Greek Cypriot, she spent her childhood in Queens inhabiting the home ground of her Greek American mother. Her existence flipped when the family returned to her father's island—trading asphalt for scented hillsides—where they lived through her teenage years.

When she leaves Cyprus to attend college in Ithaca, New York, she discovers her love of literature as a career path, the first step of her migration away from her family's expectations, but she will never cease loving her father's complicated paradise.

What binds Eleftheriou—Joanna—to Cyprus is the same pull that bound her father. "I look back now and consider," she writes, "the way that at ten, I felt I was arriving home to a place I had never seen—as if my father's home had lurked in some inherited recess of my imagination. This place was in my dreams and in my blood; it held my father's story and the story of his father before him" (26).

This beautiful book is dense with complex political history and lush topography as well as desire for both home and (eventually) the intimate love of women. In some ways the text is a classic memoir of place, reminiscent of books like Jill Ker Conway's *The Road from Coorain* and Andre Aciman's *My Alexandria.* Eleftheriou explores the deep divisions of a land that was a colony of the British Crown and is now the contested territory of two nations, as well as her immigrant father's overwhelming desire to return to a landscape that had become illumined by separation and the embellishment of memory. As in other memoirs of place that help define this genre, the narrator's hands in the raw earth are both literal and an archeological metaphor, the ground holding evidence of generations. But her divisions surpass that of ethnicity and geographical citizenship and some of the power of this book is its embrace of the erotic as well as the genealogical body. In lines reminiscent of the Greek lesbian poet Olga Broumas, the body she describes coming to attention, baking in the Cypriot sunshine or dancing to a Greek drum, is the same body that craves a woman's touch.

Music, legacy, and family story is what keeps pulling her back to the island her father kept leaving and returning to, even as another story, her own story, chills her sense of belonging to the home that doesn't have a space for her adult longings and aspirations. In the first 175 pages of the book we learn about the island's divisive politics and dangerous internal borders. We also learn about the violent Cyprus sunshine, and her father's fervent desire that she marry the son of a man to whom he owed an emotional debt.

Through her slowly unpeeling stories and ruminations, we come to understand her alliance to the romance and agricultural demands of the carob bean, and hear her when she tells us "Men slide off me like so much rainwater" (57). We learn of the father's death and the intimate village rituals she must come back from America to attend to, and we learn of her mother's quick departure back to New York, once her husband's life no longer holds her to land surrounded by the sea. We learn how Greek music, especially dancing to Greek music, collapses Joanna's conflicted sense of belonging, and we sink with her into nuanced reflections on the ways her Cypriot identity, and dialect, reshapes again when she is teaching the Greek language to American writers on retreat in Greece. We feel her visceral attachment to her Orthodox faith, as well as the severing conflicts between religion and her own becoming.

Early in the book we also see her see women, before she fully sees herself, women who are for her another beloved and stormy island. "I know the corners of her beauty," she writes of her childhood friend Erika (in an essay homage, much warmer than the original, to "He and I," the Italian writer Natalia Ginzburg's charged and cranky paean to the tiny tensions of a long marriage). Such attention to lifelong friendship with women has always been a marker of lesbian longing, such as we see in this memory of "… the precise proportionality of torso and thigh, the perfected arch of her eyebrows, and the endless tempest in her eyes"(57). The erotic charge between herself and other girls is present from the start, but she does not yet have the words to fully name herself. In the final third of the collection, the partitions of her story come together, though by this point even Erika is unsurprised at what Joanna is at last able to say aloud, and on the page—that she is a

Cypriot woman who loves women, a Cypriot Greek American Gay Woman.

It's this same friend Erika who stands in when Joanna is unable to leave her American teaching job in the States to attend the first Cyprus Pride March, their old friendship deepening into an even more intimate ally-ship at this necessary point of public and personal change. As Cyprus opens a bit, so does the author, finally able to see the history of the land and the history of lesbians as her birthright and inheritance. She even travels that 500 miles between Cyprus and Lesbos, to be present in a Greek place where lesbians gather, in order to push further into herself:

> All my life I followed the rules of my religion and culture and for many years did not speak about love. Now I have words for my desire. I call myself gay because I have been undone over and over by the beauty of a woman, years of successive, secret crushes, girl after girl, since the first erotic thrill (217).

She doesn't find a destination for her desire in Lesbos, but the act of merging place with self carries her closer.

This Way Back is precise in its attentions, but epic in its scope, reminding us of the deep intersectionality of all our queer identities. These essays show us the ways those places that make us also have the power to remake us, but only if we come back to them with all that our bodies know.

BOLD Ideas, ESSENTIAL Reading

"I remember Sahara as a spring in the desert of the time!"
—Gloria Steinem

"Leslie's tribute to Sahara is testimony to the sanctuary we found in being together, feeling safe and enthralled by a sense of freedom. Whether you found that in The Duchess, Bonnie and Clyde's or The Cubbyhole, this is your invitation to revisit. Little compared with the sense of anticipation you felt walking through the door and into the glances, stares or smiles of women and that the next few hours held countless possibilities."
—Ginny Apuzzo, gay rights and AIDS activist and former executive director of the National LGBTQ Task Force

"Beautifully written....
I love Leslie's book.
The detail she gives is remarkable both about her relationship with Beth, the beginning of Sahara where I spent many an amazing evening, and even her days in Siena. Leslie brings it all back to life. Reading this book, I was brought back to the Upper East Side in the '70s. Leslie had a magnetic power, and it suffuses the pages of this book."
—Brenda Feigen, feminist activist, film producer, attorney, cofounder of *Ms. Magazine*

"Bold, beautiful and brutally honest. [Cohen] writes as she has lived, without fear or hesitation."
—Brooke Kennedy, Emmy Award nominated television producer and director

"Sahara was the only female place that I felt comfortable as I identified with the atmosphere and the women who patronized it—fashionable, glamorous, and happy."
—Patricia Field, Emmy Award-winning costume designer, stylist and fashion designer

THE AUDACITY OF A KISS
Love, Art, and Liberation
Leslie Cohen
$24.94 cloth

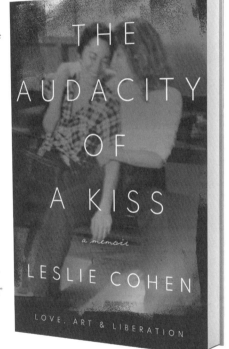

THE AUDACITY OF A KISS

a memoir

LESLIE COHEN

LOVE, ART & LIBERATION

RUTGERS
UNIVERSITY PRESS

30% off and free shipping. Use code RLCOHEN.
Discount valid sitewide.
www.rutgersuniversitypress.org

Sinister Wisdom
A Multicultural Lesbian Literary & Art Journal

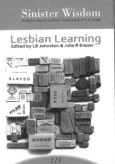

Sinister Wisdom

Lesbian Learning
Edited by LB Johnston & Julie R Enszer

118

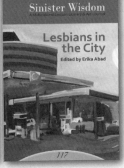

Sinister Wisdom

Lesbians in the City
Edited by Erika Abad

117

SUBSCRIBE TODAY!

Subscribe using the enclosed subscription card or online at
www.SinisterWisdom.org/subscribe using PayPal

Or send check or money order to
Sinister Wisdom - 2333 McIntosh Road, Dover, FL 33527-5980

Sinister Wisdom accepts gifts of all sizes to support the journal.

Sinister Wisdom is free on request to women in prisons
and psychiatric institutions.

Back issues available!

Sinister Wisdom **Back Issues Available**

122 Writing Communities ($14)

121 Eruptions of Inanna ($17.95)

120 Asian Lesbians ($14)

119 To Be a Jewish Dyke in the 21st
Century ($14)

118 Forty-five Years: A Tribute to the
Lesbian Herstory Archives ($14)

116 Making Connections ($14)

114 A Generous Spirit ($18.95)

108 For The Hard Ones.
Para las duras ($18.95)

107 Black Lesbians—
We Are the Revolution! ($14)

104 Lesbianima Rising: Lesbian-Feminist
Arts in the South, 1974–96 ($12)

103 Celebrating the Michigan Womyn's
Music Festival ($12)

102 The Complete Works of Pat Parker
($22.95)
    Special Limited edition hardcover($35)

98 Landykes of the South ($12)

96 What Can I Ask ($18.95)

93 Southern Lesbian-Feminist
Herstory 1968–94 ($12)

91 Living as a Lesbian ($17.95)

88 Crime Against Nature ($17.95)

80 Willing Up and Keeling Over

58 Open Issue

54 Lesbians & Religion

50 Not the Ethics Issue

49 The Lesbian Body

48 Lesbian Resistance Including
work by Dykes in Prison

47 Lesbians of Color: Tellin' It
Like It 'Tis

46 Dyke Lives

45 Lesbians & Class (the first issue of a
lesbian journal edited entirely by
poverty and working class dykes)

43/44 15th Anniversary double-size
(368 pgs) retrospective

- Sister Love: The Letters
of Audre Lorde and Pat Parker ($14.95)

- Notes for a Revolutión ($14)

Sister Love:
The Letters of Audre Lorde
and Pat Parker
1974 - 1989

Introduction by Mecca Jamilah Sullivan
Edited by Julie R. Enszer

Back issues are $6.00
unless noted plus $3.00
Shipping & Handling
for 1st issue; $1.00 for each
additional issue.
Order online at
www.sinisterwisdom.org

Or mail check or money
order to:
Sinister Wisdom
2333 McIntosh Road
Dover, FL 33527-5980